Answered -OR- Unanswered?

Answered

-OR-

Unanswered?

Miracles of Faith in China

by

Louisa Vaughan

SCRIPTURE TESTIMONY EDITION

WALKING TOGETHER PRESS

ESTES PARK · JENTA MANGORO

About the cover: This image is a scene of terraced rice fields outside a Chinese village around 1920. This would be a typical view for Louisa Vaughan.

This image is in the public domain.

Village and Terraced Fields, Ing Tai, Fujian, China, Ca. 1920. 1910. https://collections.library.yale.edu/catalog/11420754. (accessed June 17, 2024)

Colorized by Jacoba Looije

© 2024 Walking Together Press

Published in 2024 by
Walking Together Press
Estes Park, Colorado USA
Jenta Mangoro, Jos, Plateau Nigeria
https://walkingtogether.press

ISBN: 978-1-961568-02-0

Answered or Unanswered is in the public domain
Text from 1920 edition published by Christian Life Literature Fund, Philadelphia

Scripture Testimony Index content © 2024 Walking Together Press, all rights reserved

Cover design by D. Thaine Norris
Typeset in Adobe Garamond Pro by D. Thaine Norris

About the Scripture Testimony Edition

L OUISA VAUGHAN was a Presbyterian missionary in China from 1896 to 1912. She lived in the present reality of God, and wrote this beautiful and engaging collection of stories testifying to that reality. Two subjects of faith recur in almost every story; that the believer can ask anything in the name of Jesus, and that via prayer and repentance, genuine revival comes through a visitation of the Holy Spirit.

Data science reveals trends and patterns in information. The Scripture Testimony Index is an extensive research project using artificial intelligence and data science to develop a New-Testament driven subject index across a large body of missionary biographies and personal narratives. As the story enthusiasts at Walking Together Press study these books programmatically; beautiful, bright threads emerge—threads of prayer, provision, deliverance, specific leading, healing, transformation, revival, and miraculous conversion. The end result is an index of thousands of short story excerpts organized by subject and Bible verse that empirically demonstrate the truth of the Scriptures, and which is freely available on our website at walkingtogether.life. Another result of this research was the discovery of dozens of great books that are long out of print and in danger of being forgotten. The Scripture Testimony Collection is a set of such books that we enthusiastically recommend, to the degree that we are making the effort to republish them.

Walking Together Press has enhanced this classic title, *Answered OR Unanswered? Miracles of Faith in China*, by identifying and marking twenty-five portions of the narrative that illustrate specific Biblical topics and verses. A *Scripture Testimony Index* has also been added containing short summaries of how each Scriptural topic is illustrated, making locating specific stories easy. Furthermore, this title is one of many in the *Scripture Testimony Collection.*

This Book is gratefully and lovingly
DEDICATED
To Dr. and Mrs. C. E. Bradt and the friends in
The First Presbyterian Church
of Wichita, Kansas, U. S. A.,
Who so loyally supported the writer with both
their prayers and their gifts,
Thus enabling her to serve God by her faith and
testimony in China.

Preface

THE AIM of this little volume is to set forth as simply, and as concisely as possible, the incidents connected with my life and service for the Lord Jesus during my residence in China from October, 1896, to January, 1912. These stories as written were the result of the vision which the Lord Himself gave me concerning my witness-bearing amongst the Chinese people. And this testimony was to be one of Faith, based on His own promises in John 14:1, 13, 14. During this period of doubt and unbelief in the minds of many of the Lord's children I trust the stories may be a word of help and encouragement in season.

Some of the persons mentioned in the stories have already gone to be with their Master in Heaven; many still remain alive in their various churches in Shan Tung Province, North China. They can corroborate, word for word, the incidents as written in the accompanying volume.

Pastor Ding is called the Moody of China today. Rev. Swen is pastor over a large independent church in the city of Nanking. Many other workers and pastors are in other places giving their own testimony to God's grace, love and power through simple faith in His Word.

LOUISA VAUGHAN
St. Louis, Missouri

Introduction

By Charles Edwin Bradt

SOME PEOPLE tell us that the day of miracles is past. Where are such people looking, that they cannot see miracles on every hand? Miracles? Yes, miracles!— the same in kind and cause as we read of in the Bible. Save the one greatest miracle of all the ages,—Jesus Christ, whose name is Wonderful, Counsellor, the Mighty God, the Everlasting Father and the Prince of Peace, there are no Bible miracles more wonderful than those of contemporary times. What is a miracle? Prof. A. G. Hogg writes in an unusually up-to-date and scientifically scriptural manner when he says:

"Miracle and Supernatural are unsatisfactory expressions. Etymologically they express only wonder and baffled understanding. But their acquired Christian meaning is positive. They are occurrences of which the human condition is not the self-competent manipulation of ascertained means, but is a definite exertion of our trust in the Father. To base our belief in Christianity on miracle and on the supernatural in this sense of the terms need not be to base it on external evidence; on the contrary, it is to found it on what we may test in our own experience. To work miracles and make confident drafts upon the supernatural is our Christian duty and privilege. Yet miracle- working is no easy activity. It is controlled by stringent conditions. It is a grace which we earn with our whole soul's tasking."

The writer of these chapters is working on the lines of faith and prayer which lead straight to the goal of the wonderful, the operating base of every obedient Christian. Why should it be thought a thing incredible that God should raise the dead and do many other wonderful works through His faithful servants? If Christians would only obey Him, the things that Christ did would they do also and greater works than those would they do, because Christ has gone to the Father and has poured out His wonder working Spirit upon all who will respond to carry out His new and supernatural program of love, joy, peace, long-suffering, gentleness, meekness, self-control, faith, as experienced and preached by all who go with Him to give the gospel to a lost world.

In other words, Miss Vaughan believes in the efficacy of faith and prayer. But faith and prayer are just ways of obeying Jesus Christ when He says: "All authority has been given unto Me in heaven and on earth. Go ye, therefore, and make disciples of all the nations, baptizing them into the name of the Father and of the Son and of the Holy Spirit: teaching them to observe all things whatsoever I have commanded you: and lo, I am with you always, even unto the end of the world."

We invite anybody and everybody to read these personal testimonies, and then set about specifically and in harmony with God's will as revealed in His Word and His world to have similar experiences themselves. I do not mean that they should undertake to duplicate just such events as are reported here; but that they apply the principles of faith and prayer to their everyday problems, and to the issues of life as they exist, and set about righting and adjusting the wrongs and irregularities of the world in God's way. Let them do this one by one, definitely and specifically, making each one a test case before God in the laboratory of faith and prayer, and it will not be long before they will personally realize that God is our Father who hears and answers His children when they call unto Him. But let each one be fully persuaded in his own mind. Let him know that he must be a willing and obedient child ready to go with Jesus Christ unto the uttermost in the spirit and practice of the gospel for a lost world. Let him know that the sin of Selfishness, of Exclusiveness, of Racialism, of Covetousness, of Sectarianism, of Provincialism, of Pharasaism,—all sin must be confessed before God and repented of in the spirit of abandonment: and that the will to obey God in everything known to be His command and desire must be exercised to the fullest degree of purpose. Thus it was we got the story of the Acts of the first Apostles; thus it will be in the repetition of all such experiences. Are we willing to pay the price? Such experiences cost dearly. But they pay big dividends, as the following pages clearly demonstrate.

Foreword to Second Edition

By Robert C. McQuilkin

THOSE WHO were so fortunate as to secure a copy of the "twelve stories of Chinese experiences" which were included in that first small edition of "Answered or Unanswered?" recognized that they had been privileged to read a book that was truly unique among books on prayer. This new edition, which contains six additional stories, appears at a time of spiritual crisis of the Church which gives it added significance.

In a day when we are much concerned to follow the right "program" of activities for the Church, this little book on the real meaning of prayer gives a record of what happens when God's program of prayer and faith is followed. It is God and His working that is in evidence throughout these narratives of startling modern miracles. The stress is laid where the New Testament lays it—on the prayer that gets answered, the prayer that changes things. "Answered or Unanswered ?" is the challenging question that should test our petitions for God to do things. To the extent that the Church departs from the experience of Apostolic power in getting things from God, to that extent will she welcome and applaud books on prayer which beautifully discuss its philosophy and altogether omit any testimony to the kind of praying that gets miracle results. But thousands today who are true to the "old paths" will be grateful for this testimony to Him who is the same yesterday today and forever, and who is ready to work for us as for those believing Chinese Christians.

Miss Vaughan sends forth this second edition with the prayer, "May God use these testimonies to refresh many a weary soldier of the Cross in this land, and in the foreign mission fields, by bringing through them renewed assurance of victory in 'Our Lord Jesus Christ,' He who was endued with 'all power in heaven and on earth' still occupies the seat of honor at the right hand of God, and is using that power today on behalf of those who are worthy."

In a missionary family one night we were discussing the matter of God's willingness to work real miracles on the mission field today, and I told the pioneer missionary who was present about Miss Vaughan's experiences, handing him a copy of the little book. Later in the evening I found him copying by hand the first chapter of the book. We asked him what his idea was. "This is the thing I have been looking for for years," he said. "It is the greatest single need on our mission field today to see the truth that is stated in this book more definitely than I have ever seen it expressed. We work for years and years on a mission station and do not expect any results to come except in a slow, natural way. I know that fields differ and there may be testings for years, but I have believed that the greatest hindrance to miracle results is our own lack of faith and expectancy. I want every missionary on our field to get a copy of this story."

This missionary is now back on his field, and recent reports from the director of his mission tell of new bold plans for reaching out after souls. Shall we stand back of the missionaries not only by prayer for them, but by that kind of faith in our own lives that will change things right here, and will thus enable the Spirit to use us as more effective channels to pray miracles into being on the mission field. Those who were associated with Miss Vaughan in this work in China testify that the work was truly of the Lord and marvelous in their eyes, and those of us who have known her since in America can add our testimony that the same Lord has done the same sort of things here in answer to her prayer of faith.

May the book continue its gracious ministry of stirring up the Lord's own children to a new boldness in claiming things from the mighty Lord who waits to bless, and may its author soon have her heart's desire, if it be for His glory, to return to her beloved China where she may believe Him for still greater working.

Contents

Answered -OR- Unanswered?

Chapter I

My First Bible Class in China

IN CHINA, in the spring of nineteen hundred and three, I held my first Bible class for women inquirers. Having spent five years in the study of the language and in teaching in Christian work, I was delighted to find myself in a position where it was possible to bring the blessed gospel of the grace of God to my Chinese sisters.

In the little village of Dung Kia An, hid away in the heart of the beautiful Lao mountains, the Chinese pastor has gathered together twenty-five women, as an inquirers' class, that I might instruct them. In a ten- day school session I was to give them a saving knowledge of the Truth. I assumed that they all could read, at least a little, and I had bright hopes of what I should be able to do for them.

But as I talked personally with the members of my class those bright hopes died. One informed me that I could teach her nothing, her heart and mind were as hard and dark as mahogany wood. The next one said that she knew nothing; that she had never learned a thing in her life; and anyway how could she be expected to study with her children to care for, one a baby in her arms and the other a little one of three at her side? Following her came a woman of more than sixty years. As she talked to me she wiped her eyes with her sleeve.

"It was very nice of you to come to teach us, Miss Vaughan, but I can't learn; I'm too old. Besides I have cried day and night since I was thirteen and went to my mother-in-law's home and now my eyes are ruined." (Many Chinese women cry themselves blind before they are forty years old.) "I can see nothing clearly, how can I see to read books?"

All of the members of the class were in practically the same condition. They had never been to school, they did not know one character of their language from another and they were sure they could not learn— they had been taught from childhood that they had no brains. Every one of them had bound feet and the constant pain detracted their attention from everything they tried to do.

A more discouraged teacher than I, at the end of my roll call, it would have been difficult to find. I said to myself, "How can these women be taught? They have come to me because their pastor has sent them. Their minds are wholly undeveloped and they have not even a wish to improve."

Utterly dismayed at the task before me, I went to my room to pray. There had been a very insistent question in my heart, "Where is your faith in God?"

What has faith to do with this ? I answered, "This is my task and it is humanly impossible."

"With men this is impossible; but with God all things are possible," came the answer to my argument.

I dropped to my knees, confessing my spiritual ignorance and helplessness, and prayed that God would show me exactly what that passage meant.

Immediately, like a flash of light in a dark room, came these two promises: "And whatsoever ye shall ask in My name that will I do, that the Father may be glorified

> ### SCRIPTURE TESTIMONY
> *Ask Me anything in My name*
>
> MATTHEW 18:19 ·
> JOHN 14:13-14 · JOHN 16:23-24

in the Son. If ye shall ask anything in my name, I will do it." (John 14:13-14.)

My burden rolled away as I realized the full import of these gracious words. I had nothing to do but to ask, for the Omnipotent God, my Saviour and the Saviour of these women, He who had died for us, had promised to do for me whatever I asked. I knew not how nor when, but He would fulfill His promise.

I felt in my heart the truth of these words:

> *"We are coming to a King,*
> *Large petitions will we bring."*

I made no small request; I asked the Father to forgive them for Jesus' sake, to pour out His Holy Spirit upon them, convincing them of sin, of righteousness and of the world to come; to reveal to them the Lord Jesus Christ as their personal Saviour; to cleanse them in His precious blood from the guilt and stain of sin; and finally to fill them with His Holy Spirit that they might return to their homes to witness for Jesus.

Back to this class of illiterate women, bound in chains of iron by their superstitions, I went rejoicing in the Lord who had made such abundant provision for bringing the world to Himself, and resolved to wait patiently for Him to perform His miracle in each of their darkened and sinful hearts.

Meanwhile I taught them this prayer: "Heavenly Father, forgive me my sins, cleanse me from them in the precious blood of Christ, and fill me with the Holy Spirit; I ask in Jesus' name."

Some of the women spent the greater part of three days in learning correctly and intelligently this very simple petition.

My first day with them passed slowly, with no sign from God that He had heard my prayer. Throughout the next morning there was still no evidence that He was working. But that afternoon while we were on our knees repeating together the little prayer, one of the women began to weep out a confession of her sins. She asked that she might be forgiven and cleansed in the precious blood and that the Holy Spirit would come into her heart and dwell there. In a few moments we rose from our knees to greet a new creature in Christ Jesus. In the course of the next few days woman followed woman in a similar experience until the entire class rejoiced in their salvation. They were marvelously transformed by the power of the Holy Spirit, for they were now so eager to learn of Christ that I could scarcely find time to satisfy them. My strength was taxed to the utmost in giving them the help and teaching they sought.

During the next ten years of my residence in China. I held five or six classes of this kind annually. I always claimed those promises of John 14:13-14 and trusted in God to do the work in response to the prayer of faith. I do not know of one, in all this time, who left my classes unsaved.

In one village where I was teaching a heathen woman came to hear me out of curiosity to see a white woman who could speak the Chinese language. After listening to the little prayer which I was teaching she asked if she might learn I answered, "Would you like to have a Saviour and are you willing to accept Him?"

She said yes and became a member of my class. In the afternoon she returned and took her place with the others. When the invitation was given for all to kneel in prayer, to my astonishment, this woman, Mrs. Wang, began to sob, confessing her sins and pleading with the Lord to forgive her and to cleanse her heart and save her.

That same evening I gave the women John 14:13-14 and told them that these promises were their inheritance. Then I asked them what they wished to pray for.

Mrs. Wang stood up and asked, "Can the Lord Jesus save my husband?"

I told her that He was the omnipotent God.

"Oh," she said, "but you don't know my husband; he is a drunkard. I've never known him to come home sober since I married him. I'm forty-five now and I went to my mother-in-law's a bride of less than fourteen years. He spends so much money for drink that the children and I never have enough to eat, nor warm clothing enough to keep us comfortable in winter. Can the Lord Jesus save a man like that, Miss Vaughan?"

"Yes," I replied, "He came to seek and to save that which was lost."

Then I asked of her, "Can you believe?"

She burst into tears, "Oh, yes, but I'm so ignorant. I don't know how to pray. Won't you pray for me?"

I put the matter before the class, telling them we must be agreed to pray every day for this man until he was converted. This we did for two weeks, at the end of which time the class had to be disbanded that I might go on with my work in other territory.

A year later I returned to this district. The morning my class opened Mrs. Wang was among the first arrivals. Rushing in and throwing her arms around me, she praised God for His goodness to her.

"Please, Miss Vaughan," she said, "ask the women to sit down while I tell them what the Lord has done."

SCRIPTURE TESTIMONY
Father forgive them, for they know not what they do
LUKE 23:34 · ACTS 7:60

This was her story: "A year ago, at the close of the class in which I learned to know my Saviour, I went home and told my husband I had become a Christian. He was furiously angry and beat me so that I was not able to leave my kang* for a month. During that time he reviled me and cursed me every day. I had only my little son to prepare my food and care for me. When I was well my husband continued to persecute me for six months. All the time I prayed for him constantly. I just asked God to forgive him because he didn't understand.

"And then one day he came home early from a neighboring market, sober for the first time since I had known him.

"'What is the matter with you?' I cried in astonishment.

"'That's what I came to ask you,' he replied. 'What is the matter with me? Am I out of my mind?'

"Why, I said, 'what has happened?'

"'A great deal,' he answered. 'Today when I had finished my business in the market I went across to the wine shop, and just as I was lifting my foot over the threshold, a voice inside my body said very loudly, "Don't go in there, go home! Don't go in there, go home!" I was so startled that I dropped my purse and spilled all my coins on the ground.

"I tried to make myself quiet by thinking that it must have been some boys making fun of me. I went across the street and searched a man's courtyard and looked carefully around the corners of his

---

*   A kang (pronounced kong) is the mud brick platform covered with straw matting where the entire family sleeps.

house to find the boys who had called to me. I looked up and down the street, but there was not a soul in sight. There were many men in the wine shop, though; I could hear their voices and what they said. I walked over there again. I was very much puzzled and called myself a fool. But again as I lifted my foot over the threshold there came that voice, louder and more insistent than ever: "Don't go in there, go home! Don't go in there, go home!" I came right home as fast as I could. I am very much frightened. Do you think I am losing my mind, or am I already mad? What is the matter with me?'

"'Oh,' I said, 'I know what's the matter. That's the Lord Jesus. He is the heavenly Father's Son. He died on the cross to save you. He does not want you to go in the wine shop and get drunk and be lost. It is the voice of His Holy Spirit speaking to you.'

"He was astounded. He listened intently while I told him over and over again that Jesus was his Saviour.

"Finally he said, 'Is this that Devil's doctrine you learned at Tai Tze Dswang?'

"'Not the Devil's doctrine, the Jesus doctrine.'

"'Well,' he said, 'why didn't you tell me this before? I didn't understand. I'll never drink any more in my life.'"

And he never did. He was truly converted. He became a member of the church and induced his family to become members also, and sent his children to a Christian school.

She lived four years after his conversion and died a blessed, happy Christian, rejoicing in Jesus and His power to save. Her husband, at this writing, is alive still.

Chapter II

Ding Le Mei

IN THE winter of 1903-4, the Mission transferred me from Chefoo to the new German port of Tsing Tau, where I was placed in charge of the women's work of the fifteen organized churches scattered through the adjoining counties. In other words, to me was given the oversight of the Bible women, girls' schools and prospective church members.

I had not been long in my new work when the pastors, and some of the elders, held a conference relating to the spiritual needs in the various fields in their district. I was asked to describe the methods I used with the women, which resulted in such spiritual enlightenment for them.

"I depend not upon any method," I replied, "but upon the power of the Holy Spirit."

"But we haven't this power," they informed me.

"No," I said, "it comes only in response to prayer and faith. The three things always go together— prayer, faith, and power. Do you want this power ?"

They said that there was nothing they wanted more.

9

"Then," I asked, "would you be willing to form, with me, a circle in which we shall pray daily, first for ourselves and then for each other?"

Eight of them gladly agreed to do so.

Our plan was simple and direct.

Our prayer was, "Heavenly Father, forgive me my sins; send the Holy Spirit into my heart to reveal them to me; cleanse me from them in the precious blood of Jesus, and fill me with Thy Spirit." This each offered daily for six months.

Pastor Ding Le Mei, a member of our circle, who had been called to the five Chi Mo churches, wrote to me at the end of the six months. He invited me to assist him in conducting a four-day conference for deepening the spiritual life of the Chinese Christians under his charge, and I accepted his invitation.

I arrived at the little village of Yuen Dswang at ten o'clock on the morning of the first day of the conference. The meetings had begun, but, alas, for human plans! It has been-said that man proposes and God disposes, but on that day Satan disposed.

Funeral services fast for days or weeks, according to the rank or riches of the deceased. A very wealthy man in the village had just died, and arrangements had been made to observe his obsequies throughout all the days of the conference. As I passed along the street I saw piles of paper money, paper cows, horses, sedan chairs, slaves,—everything that the departed spirit would need in the next world, ready to be burned at the burial. Groups of people were sending up skyrockets to scare away the evil spirits. Everywhere where were evidences of the importance of the occasion; and everywhere absorbing interest and excitement were apparent.

There may be theatres in China that are wholly secular in character, but all about which I know are connected with religious worship, and appropriately, therefore, with funeral observances. Now, in the temple theatre a company of actors had been hired, and as the performance was free to all, it and the other features of the celebration had attracted immense crowds from the neighboring villages.

These people, unaccustomed to listening to lectures or talks of any kind, made their way by hundreds into the conference tent, talking at the top of their voices, their babies crying and the village dogs barking at their heels. We Christian women, for whom a remote corner of the tent had been roped off, not only could not catch the air of the songs, but not one word that was said or sung could we distinguish during the course of the day.

This noise and confusion, impossible to control, brought grief and dismay to Pastor Ding.

At the close of the afternoon session, the officers and leaders of his churches went to him in anger and reproached him for his lack of discretion in selecting such an inopportune season for the conference; and they gave him to understand that they did not propose to waste any more time or money on it and would leave the village the next morning by dawn.

Pastor Ding was the first Chinese pastor to step out, with faith in God, in any enterprise financed by the Chinese Christians. To these men he was looking for financial help. His own salary was too meagre to defray the expenses already incurred. In despair he came to me with his difficulty.

"I already realize what the conditions are and there is only one person who can deal with them," I said. "There is just one person who can turn defeat into victory. That is the Lord and we'll just ask Him to do this very thing for us."

Pastor Ding's father and grandfather were Christians, and he had been brought up in the Christian quarter of his village. He loved his Saviour and was a man of prayer,-but he knew nothing of the "exceeding greatness of God's power to usward who believe" and exercise faith in Christ.

We knelt in prayer for a few minutes, but we were not of one mind in the Lord. He asked God to give me a plan that I might give it to him. In other words, he wanted a plan that would enable him to turn his own defeat into victory. Then he sat waiting for me to tell him what to do. I, of course, waited only for Christ to answer the prayer that He had promised to answer. (John 14:13-14.) We sat thus for an hour, while my Chinese servant worked himself into quite a fever because I took no notice of the over-cooked supper.

Finally Pastor Ding arose, and Chinese etiquette demanded that I, being a woman, should stand also. So we stood for half an hour. Then I flew in the face of Chinese convention and asked him to take supper with me. Declining my invitation, his face flushed with anger and impatience, and, slamming the door behind him, he left me.

(Afterward he told me that he mutered to himself, "That's what I get for asking a woman anything! What does she know ?")

I saw him again at the evening service where he was presiding. As we had only Christian men and women in the audience, all was quiet and orderly. The unconverted Chinese stayed at home because of their fear of evil spirits in the darkness of the night.

We had prayers, songs and the reading of the Scriptures. Pastor Ding was about to give out the text of his address, when the Holy Spirit prompted me to rise and ask, "Won't you give us five minutes for personal prayer? And let each one pray, 'Heavenly Father, forgive me my sins, send the Holy Spirit into my heart and reveal them to me. Cleanse me from them in the precious blood and fill me with Thy Spirit.'"

He consented rather reluctantly, but he repeated my request and added: "Let us kneel and offer this prayer together."

Then a wonderful thing occurred. The Holy Spirit came upon the Assembly so suddenly and with such mighty power, that before their knees touched the floor, they were all, as with one

SCRIPTURE TESTIMONY
Holy Spirit directs believers in ministry
MATTHEW 10:19-20 · ACTS 8:29 · ACTS 13:2 · ACTS 15:28 · ACTS 16:6-10 · ACTS 20:22 · ROMANS 8:14
Holy Spirit convicts people of their sin
JOHN 16:8

voice, sobbing aloud their sins of omission and commission, sins of neglect of the spiritual lives of their children, of not loving one another and not loving God, sins of quarrelling, of covetousness, of hatred, and of Sabbath breaking.

The men who, in the afternoon had gone with complaints to Pastor Ding, now weeping, called upon God to deliver them from covetousness. They had made the failure of the meeting an excuse to leave when their real reason was to avoid their share of defraying the expense. Thus in a few moments God had swept all difficulties away. He had truly turned defeat into victory.

For more than half an hour the confessions continued. Then we stood up and sang four times the hymn which begins,

> "There is a fountain filled with blood
> Drawn from Emmanuel's veins,"

I shall never forget that singing nor that scene— those upturned, tear stained Chinese faces with the light of heaven upon them.

Then came more confessions, testimonies, prayer and praise unceasing, for two hours.

Pastor Ding tried again and again to preach the sermon he had prepared, but he never got a chance. When at last, near the close of the meeting, he secured a hearing, he told of his interview with me. He had confessed to God his lack of faith. And he asked my pardon for his rudeness. Then, turning to his people, he begged their forgiveness for attempting to lead them in his own blindness. "And," he added, "I call you, Miss Vaughan, and you, my brothers and sisters, to witness that I promise never again to use in God's service, any method save that of prayer and faith. Tonight I have seen the mighty power of God in answer to prayer and I rejoice."

During the remaining days of the conference, the Holy Spirit held control, and though we had the same great crowds from the theatre, they sat or stood quietly throughout the service. Every speaker was heard distinctly, even in the women's remote corner.

And God's gracious purpose of blessing by means of the Conference had been fully accomplished. Chinese Christians and leaders who had come to us from a distance returned home, their hearts and minds full of the glory of God's goodness and power. Everywhere they proclaimed the news of our great answers to prayer and requests for similar meetings began to pour in. Pastor Ding and I responded as fully as our physical strength permitted. For seven months we went from Conference to Conference, returning home only for brief preparations for starting out anew. At every Conference the Spirit was poured out in power and blessing, as fully as at Yuen Dswang.

Pastor Ding Le Mei had entered upon his life work as an evangelist. Later on he accepted an invitation to tour Shan Tung

Province and everywhere God manifested his power by means of his servant's faith. Later still the Young Men's Christian Association arranged for him to visit all the schools, colleges, and universities throughout China. God has so marvelously empowered him that he is known today as the "Apostle of China," and "China's Moody."

Chapter III

The Other Six

THE SERIES of meetings held in Yuen Tswang village the opening night at which Pastor Ding Le Mei received his vision of God's power through faith, was the beginning of an outpouring of God's Holy Spirit, on the Christians in this part of the province such as had never before been witnessed in China. We had a great revival. For seven months of that memorable year, my fellow workers Ding Le Mei, and Twen Itsi Sing and I went from church to church, and from village to village, rejoicing in seeing the same power in evidence everywhere, wonderful conviction of sin, deep contrition, lively repentance.

The prayer life of Christians during those days was remarkable, some of our prayer meetings continuing for seven hours at a stretch. It was a common happening to pray for half the night.

Backsliders were restored, sin was uncovered and confessed, the sick were healed, and the efficacy of the blood of the Lord Jesus Christ was demonstrated in power.

This little book contains a few, just a few, of the most remarkable wonders God did for us during those days. Even as of old, if all was written all the books in the world would not contain the stories of the wonders of His grace.

SCRIPTURE TESTIMONY
Generously give to those in need
ACTS 4:32-37 · GALATIANS 6:2 · HEBREWS 13:16 · I JOHN 3:17

A remarkable result of the revival was the conviction of the sins of coveteousness amongst the Chinese Christians, the confession and cleansing of these sins, and a liberality of giving most astonishing. At one time I had piled up in a large heap on a table before me an offering from the women, consisting of rings, earrings, bracelets, ornaments for the hair and charms. In many cases the women gave their wedding rings. When they had nothing more to give they donated their time, some giving a day each week to preach the Gospel, some half a day, some a week each month, some a month and two months each half year, until we had so much time donated it would have taken thousands of dollars to have paid for it in cash.

One heathen woman in Tsing Tau was saved and she came to me with a proposition that if I would take a trip with her she would pay all her own expenses and take me into a dozen villages where she had relatives, none of whom had heard the Gospel. Of course I went, and we had blessed results. God's power and grace everywhere prevailed.

I have been asked, "Was the prayer of your circle of eight as abundantly answered for the six others as it was for you and Pastor Ding?"

Elder Liu came to a realization of his wonderful privilege in using his means for Christ. At one time he gave four thousand dollars in gold, the largest gift from a Chinese Christian ever known in that part of the country.

Elder Ding increased his contribution to the Chinese Church ten-fold and for years gave his services as Principal of the Girls' School at Ta Shun Tan. During all this time he taught two advanced classes, daily.

Pastor Swen, who at the time of our prayers had the care of three churches which had recanted during the Boxer uprising, was enabled under God to restore them from their backsliding. He was "thoroughly furnished" spiritually for the enlarged work and responsibility to which he was afterward called when he became pastor of the Chinese church in the Southern Capital, Nanking. Of this church, one of our most important mission centers, he is still in charge.

Elder Tsiao and his wife were so blessed in their new vision that they dedicated to the use of The Women's Bible Training School a house of fourteen rooms. This house was used during the six years of my principalship, free of rent. During all this time Mrs. Tsaio gave her services as matron.

The value of the testimony of these two to the students of the Training School is beyond human reckoning.

I have not kept in touch with Pastor Tung and do not know the details of his experience. I do know, however, that his blessing was great.

Chapter IV

A First Venture in Faith

LIFE IN China as it presents itself to a single woman missionary who has been born and bred in the Occident is decid-
edly a complex tangle.* In the first place, she cannot live
without a servant, cannot travel without him, cannot market
without him. He must be had
at all costs. So, according to
custom, a servant I had to
have. This person, so necessary to my wellbeing, was
found in a Christian Chinese,

SCRIPTURE TESTIMONY
Deliverance from enemies and circumstances
LUKE 1:71

Shao Wei Chao, from a tiny village in the southern part of Shan
Tung Province. He was a tall, good looking man, with rosy
cheeks; he had a wife, two children, and a mother to support.
Shao Wei Chao was perfectly innocent of the art of cooking, but

---

* Editor's Note,—This incident occurred when Miss Vaughan
was appointed to take charge of the women's work in the Che Moa
churches and previous to her remarkable experience as recorded in
Chapter I

21

was willing to learn, and with very little ado he was engaged to cook. Or, as his official title described him, "Ta Si Fu," "The Great Father of Affairs"; in plain English, "The great business manager."

Equipped with this wonderful personality, and a Bible woman, I was ready to go anywhere or do anything.

Shao Wei Chao had been with me about a year, when during the Summer while I was busy preparing my winter's work, he fell in with a group of men in Chefoo who led him astray. They persuaded him that he could earn much more money serving some Russian officer in Port Arther than in working for me. So one day he told me he had decided to set out for that city in a few days.

Realizing the conditions there and knowing some of the wrecked lives resulting from Russian civilization, I felt it my duty and privilege to take him to God in prayer.

I spent three days praying. I do not mean I knelt and prayed and did nothing else; I mean my time in which I was not eating or teaching, I spent in prayer for this one thing.

I asked the Lord to prevent his going to this city, to bring him back, and save him. Three weeks passed. I heard nothing; then accidentally meeting one of my fellow-workers one morning she said, "Do you know that your cook has returned ?"

My heart sang for joy. I knew my Lord had heard and answered my prayer. His story was interesting beyond words. I shall give it as he related it to me:

"The day we left Chefoo we engaged a junk to sail across the strait. The weather was delightful, a favorable wind blowing our ship directly toward Port Arthur. In a few hours we were in the harbour so close to land we could see the houses and almost hear the people talk as they walked on the Bund. We prepared to land, but in an instant, without the slightest warning, the wind veered and blew from the shore so fiercely that in a few minutes we were out at sea again, and in the midst of a raging storm. For three days and three nights without food or water we expected each moment to be our last. Before our eyes a larger junk, filled with Japanese traders, overturned in the angry sea and every soul perished. We could render no aid, but expected each moment to be engulfed in similar fashion. I cried to my Heavenly Father, 'Lord save us,' and he heard me.

"We were blown back across the strait into the Harbour of Wei Hai Wei, a few miles south of Chefoo. We disembarked more dead than alive, found an inn, spent days and nights waiting for the wind to change so we could set out once more for Port Arthur.

"Finally that day arrived. Early in the morning we tied our belongings in bags. With these on our shoulders we soon were on our way to the dock. One of my friends said, 'We are starting out again without any food. Suppose, Sao Si Fu, you give me your bag and you run down the street and buy some hard tack.' Very innocently I handed to him my 'all my possessions.' Having bought the food I returned to the dock, but found no junk. Alarmed, I called loudly. My voice came back over the sea, mocking me. The boat was already under sail and at least two hundred yards from shore. My money! my clothes! my all! tied up in that bag and a great strip of water ever widening between me and my posessions. Despair seized me. I wept! I called! I begged

> **SCRIPTURE TESTIMONY**
>
> *God answers prayer*
>
> LUKE 18:7 · JOHN 15:7 ·
> ACTS 12:5 · JAMES 5:15
>
> *Don't be anxious, instead make requests known to God*
>
> PHILIPPIANS 4:6

other boatmen to overtake them, but in vain. I had no money, and they knew it. Blinded by my tears, staggering like an old man, I made my way up the street. It was then the Holy Spirit reminded me of you, Han Ku Niang. In any calamity, you always prayed.

"'Lord help me!' I cried, as I walked along and wept. Suddenly I remembered a friend's son who live in Wei-Hai-Wai. Continuing, I besought the Lord to let me find Tswang-I-Nien's son, the friend who lived here. This petition I kept repeating as I made my way up the street.

"In the distance I saw a peddler carrying his pack. Oh, I thought, he will know all the people, and where they live. I shall ask him for information. Accosting him, I ventured, after oriental etiquette had been satisfied, to enquire if he knew a man called "Tswang" the son of a cook in Chefoo, one who lived many years in the Mission Compound on Temple Hill.

"'What is your business with him, may I ask?' said the peddler.

"'I am in great trouble,' I answered, 'and I seek his help. If you can give me any information, give it to me, for I must die if I do not find someone to help me.'

"'Strange, indeed,' said the peddler, 'it should be so. I am the man you seek! The son of Tswang- I-Nien of Chefoo, Nan Lo, Temple Hill. What can I do for you?'

"In a few minutes the tale was told. The peddler took me home and kept me for several days, till I found work and Earned enough money to repay Tswang and provide for my journey back to Chefoo."

Mistakes acknowledged, faults confessed, should have only one result amongst Christians, that the erring one should be forgiven and restored. I therefore reinstated Sao-Si-Fu in his former position, in which he served me faithfully and well for seven years, growing in grace and the knowledge of the Lord Jesus Christ, bearing in his life the fruit of the Spirit, taking his place as a Christian leader in the church where he belonged as well as in the churches he visited with me.

In praying for this humble Christian servant, I began to learn one of the great lessons God had still to teach me of His power if I obeyed and trusted Him.

Chapter V

The Farmer's Tenth

Will a man rob God? Yet ye have robbed me. But ye say,
wherein have we robbed thee? In tithes and offerings.
Ye are cursed with a curse; for ye have robbed me,
even this whole nation.
Bring ye all the tithes into the storehouse, that there
may be meat in mine house, and prove me now here-
with, saith the Lord of Hosts, if I will not open you the
windows of heaven, and pour you out a blessing, that
there shall not be room enough to receive it.
And I will rebuke the devourer for your sakes, and he
shall not destroy the fruits of your ground; neither shall
your vine cast her fruit before the time in the field, saith
the Lord of Hosts. Malachi 3: 8-11.

DURING THE revival in the Chi Moa churches the Chinese pastors were holding a conference in Yuen Tswang village, which many native Christians attended. One of the lay-brothers, Mr. Swen, had a wonderful revelation of his sins of omission,—lack of love to God and to men, lack of trust in God, disobedience to the simple and plain commandments in the New Testament, particularly in the matter of stewardship of money.

SCRIPTURE TESTIMONY
Holy Spirit convicts people of their sin
JOHN 16:8
Give and it shall be given unto you
LUKE 6:38

His repentance was deep and sincere. Standing before the assembly with tears he confessed his sins and made his vow to turn from such a course and show forth in his life that he was the Lord's true servant.

He possessed a farm of five acres, a small portion of which was devoted to raising wheat. From this small store of wheat, which he declared should be the grain presented to the Lord, he took tithe of all he possessed, and gave it to Pastor Ding Li Mei. The yield each year of wheat was about three bushels. Having discharged his debt to God, with a light heart he sowed in the fall the next year's drop, using the same amount of seed as usual, on the same sized parcel of ground. The following spring he reaped, and to his astonishment gathered into his measures four bushels of wheat. Out of the increase he put aside a tenth as a thank offering, in addition to the tenth of his old measure representing the tithe on his entire farm produce.

The second year he reaped five bushels. Delighted beyond measure, he again placed his thank offering with his tithe at his master's feet, constantly preaching Jesus as the true God to his heathen neighbors and using these facts as his testimony. The third year was best of all,—a six bushel crop without additional seed or additional land. Truly this was the Lord's power.

That year, 1907, I was on furlough in the United States. Pastor Ding had been called to tour the province in the interests of all the churches. So my friend Swen was left entirely to his own devices, perhaps, I should add, to his own and Satan's. He laid up in store his six bushels of wheat; as he said himself "Satan tempted me and I fell"; he gave no tenth that fall. He gave no thank offering.

Fall and spring came and again the reaping time. Hard of heart, and stoical, he gathered the wheat into his threshing floor, where with

SCRIPTURE TESTIMONY
Give and it shall be given unto you
LUKE 6:38

wife and son to help, beat out the grain and emptied it into the measures.

Barely three bushels! He could scarcely believe his eyes. Could it be possible? Was the great creator of the universe so exact with this tiny matter? Yes, it was even so, barely three measures of wheat.

As realization dawned his spiritual eyes were opened. He became conscious of his sin. He told me later, with the tears streaming down his face, "Satan filled my heart with covetousness. But Han Ku Niang, with God's help he shall never do so again."

Chapter VI

The Back-Slidden Church

A S STATED in the last chapter, Pastor Swen had been called to take charge of three churches, many of whose communicants had recanted during the Boxer massacres. He was much perplexed over one of them in particular, practically all of whose members had denied their Lord, in those dark and painful days. This church, the Chinese Presbytery seriously considered disbanding.

About seven months after the great out-pouring of the Spirit upon the Conference at Yuen Dswang, Mr. —, the American missionary who superintended our work, asked

> SCRIPTURE TESTIMONY
>
> *Protest against those unwilling to hear the Gospel*
>
> MATTHEW 10:14 ·
> MARK 6:11 · LUKE 9:5

me to lend Pastor Swen a helping hand. A little later I received an invitation to hold revival services ,in this difficult church, and I gladly embraced the opportunity.

In China, no respectable woman transacts any sort of business. My cook, therefore, accompanied me and beside his regular duty of preparing my meals, went to the market for food and made negotiations in the inns for donkeys or wheel barrows to carry me and my baggage from place to place.

One evening I arrived at the village of the back-slidden church. I had traveled in due state with my Bible-woman and cook in a wheel barrow. We were escorted to the home of our host, the former evangelist of this church. There my Bible-woman and I were taken to a room which opened into a hall and the hall in turn led to the street. According to Chinese convention-alities, this was no fit place for women. But worse still the place reeked with the odor of stale opium smoke. I afterwards learned that my host and some evil associates had made a compact to open this room and the others across the front of the house as a public opium den, on Chinese New Year.

While as guests, we waited for some of the Christians of the town to call upon us, we learned that the church could not be had for our services. An anti- Christian, anti-foreign teacher and his pupils already occupied it. We made inquiries as to the possibility of securing some hall in the town. None was available. The outlook for a series of revival meetings was not hopeful.

While we sat discussing our troubles we heard steps in the hall. The curtain at the door, the only shield for our privacy, was jerked aside, and some queer looking Chinese men looked in.

"Hello, what's the foreign devil doing here?" exclaimed the one who had jerked the curtain.

Another, almost hidden in smoke from his pipe, called to some one behind, "The devil's old wife is in here, let's move on."

My Bible-woman and I were much alarmed. Just then my cook came in very angry and resentful wishing to know where he was to sleep. We suggested that he ask our host for some straw in the stable.

"I have already asked him," he replied. "He says he has no straw. I just saw two large stacks in the yard. What can you do with a man like that?"

"There's nothing we can do," I answered. "Only the Lord can help us and we must ask Him to, now."

The three of us knelt in prayer, and when we arose I knew that next morning I should leave for another town. I sent the cook to a village three miles away to spend the night and to procure some wheel barrows. I knew he could not get them from the village we were stopping in.

The dawn came at last and with it the arrival of our barrows. Into them we packed our belongings with all possible speed.

The Christians of the town heard that I was leaving. Led by the one or two who had not recanted during the Boxer trouble, they gathered about me tearfully. They plead that they had been trusting God to use me in helping them, that they would never have another opportunity to be revived and that my going was a spiritual calamity. I told them that they could never have God's blessing until they repented and gave evidence of their repentance, by taking their church out of the hands of the heathen teacher and putting it again under the control of the Christians. I assured them that I would return to them as soon as possible, after they had decided to be obedient to God, and had arranged to have services in their building. I assured them that when all this had been done they might confidently expect God's blessing. Very reluctantly but very determinedly I parted from them.

As we left the village we were seen by the evangelist in whose home we had spent the night and whom Satan had used to work his will in the church. When he was told what had occurred his anger toward me knew no bounds. "Fifteen foreign missionaries have visited this church, and not one of them has treated me with such insolence and contempt," he said. "And she an unmarried woman!"

After the Boxer trouble was over, Germany, Austria, and the United States forced the Chinese government to pay indemnity to their citizens for their personal losses. This recanting evangelist had been imprisoned because of false claims at that time. Since then, three years ago, he had never opened his Bible, but in the midst of his abuse of me, he obeyed an impulse to take it from its shelf. The first words his eyes fell upon were those of Matthew 10:14. "And whosoever shall not receive you nor hear your words, when ye depart out of that house or city, shake off the dust of your feet." They were the two-edged sword of the Spirit, piercing to the very heart. He went in great distress and called the other Christians to come into the opium den where we had slept, and there with tears and prayers for forgiveness they all made their confessions to God. They then arranged to notify the non-Christian teacher and his pupils that they must vacate the church building. Later on they sent me an invitation to return to them on February 2, 1904, about three months after my first uncomfortable visit.

When I arrived, Pastor Swen, mistakenly assumed that the Christians of the congregation were now right with God personally, when they had taken only one step in repentance. He held a meeting in which he asked them to be responsible for the salary of a teacher whom he had engaged in the name of the church for a much-needed girls' school. They promptly told him that they would do nothing of the kind.

I insisted that when these people were right with God, not only as a church, but also individually, they would support this school.

He and I conducted meetings for ten days, holding sessions mornings, afternoons, and evenings. We spent many hours in praying alone or together, trusting the Holy Spirit to convict the individual Christians of their personal sins against God.

On the evening of the tenth day, shortly after the opening of the service, we gave a general invitation for prayer and confession of sin. Suddenly the evangelist, fall-

SCRIPTURE TESTIMONY
Holy Spirit convicts people of their sin JOHN 16:8

ing down on his face to the very ground, burst into tears and most agonizing sobs. When he had recovered control of his voice sufficiently to make his confession, he began at the first commandment of the Decalogue and went through the ten, confessing that he had broken them every one. Neither I nor any one else present had ever seen a human being in such mental and spiritual agony over sin. He continued to weep and pray for some time before he received the assurance of forgiveness.

Others of the congregation began to be deeply convicted of their personal sins. The soul-searching work of the Spirit continued for several days until every member of the church was restored to communion with the Lord.

Then we appointed an evening to be spent in prayer for the salary of the teacher for the girls' school.

Before I left the village the full amount was contributed, the teacher had arrived, and the school was opened. It continued to be supported by the church for two years.

The evangelist lived for four and a half years; and throughout this time was a consistent and faithful witness for the Lord Jesus Christ in what was no longer "The Back-Slidden Church," and not only there but elsewhere and to whomsoever the Lord sent him.

Chapter VII

An Evangelist's Fall

I N THE summer of 1900, Mr. Leng, a Chinese evangelist, was preaching near Tsing Tau. In company with many other Christians who were pursued by the Boxers, he had escaped to that city.

There, because of his knowledge of English, he secured a temporary position as interpreter for the German contingent going North to the relief of Tien Tsin. Finding it unsafe to return to Tsing Tau he next proceeded with the troops to Pekin.

In Pekin he indulged in resentment against the Boxers and their supporters. He forgot his Master and the grace that had redeemed him; he forgot that he was to love his enemies and pray for them that despitefully used him. Joining the foreign soldiers in looting the city, he enriched himself with goods and silver thrown into the street from burning stores and banks. He assisted in the looting of the Imperial Palace and carried off several of the Emperor's garments. For this act of vandalism he incurred the extreme penalty of the Chinese law, which provides "capital punishment of beheading" for any Chinese having in their possession any article belonging to the "Imperial family?'

He contrived in some manner to have all his booty conveyed to his own home.

Leng's ill gotten riches became his undoing. He was a terror not only to his family but to the whole village. In a drunken fury he had killed one of his own children. The neighbors finally became so much afraid that they reported his conduct to the government. The soldiers who came to arrest him searched his home and found the imperial garments. He was tried and sentenced to be beheaded.

His sentence was not executed, however, for the condemning official was suddenly removed, and in the confusion of readjustment of the Chinese government after the Boxer uprising, Leng was left a prisoner.

About a year later, I was conducting a class in the village in which Mrs. Leng lived with her children, in her mother's home. One evening Mrs. Leng, the children, and a brother of Mr. Leng, called upon me and asked me to intervene in behalf of their relative. Their idea seemed to be that as I was a member of the great Presbyterian Mission of America, it would only be necessary for me to write a letter, (with my card enclosed) asking the chief official to release Leng. In spite of my explanation they stayed until the middle of the night, pleading and weeping and even getting down on their knees to me. I assured them again and again that their plan was impossible for several reasons, but chiefly because women members of the Mission were not allowed to write letters of intercession for anyone who had disobeyed the laws of the land.

At last they became very angry and accused me of lack of love for the church members.

They were wrong, I told them. They were trusting in man's power instead of God's. After another long discussion I persuaded them to commit their trouble to the Lord. I am sure now, that they yielded not because they had faith in my plans, but because they could not induce me to promote theirs.

I told them that we must ask the Holy Spirit to reveal to us what sins of omission and commission he would have us confess, and that we must trust the Heavenly

> **SCRIPTURE TESTIMONY**
>
> *Disciples must keep their word*
>
> MATTHEW 5:37

Father to forgive and cleanse them; that we must pray for our brother Leng as a sinner and ask God to forgive his backsliding. We all agreed to offer this petition every day until the Lord heard and answered. And we kept our word.

Again a year passed by, during which God was working. A second official left his post so hurriedly that he, too, was unable to execute the death sentence on Leng.

A third official succeeded,—pro-Christian and pro- foreign. He was of the new regime in China, which finally brought about the downfall of the Manchu Dynasty. Being informed that Leng was a Christian, a man of western education and under sentence of death, he took him into his own home as tutor to his sons. Leng was most satisfactory in this capacity.

Finally a day came, when just as suddenly as the second official had been transferred, the third one also was ordered to another post. It is customary in China when a person of importance goes upon a journey, for his friends, servants, and slaves, and usually some mere hangers-on to accompany him along his way one mile, or two, or three. Leng took his place as tutor, in the procession and walked several miles by the official's sedan chair. A few at a time in the procession dropped back until only Leng was left.

The official then ordered the chair coolies to stop, and place his sedan chair on the ground, saluting Mr. Leng in Chinese style at the same time said, "thank you for your services. I hope we shall meet again and good bye!"

No word of the death sentence, no mention of return to prison. By an intentional slip the official had released him and he stood in the road alone, a free man.

In a few days, he arrived at the village where his wife and children were staying. In God's beautiful providence Pastor Ding and Pastor Swen were there conducting a Conference with the Chinese Christians.

When Mr. Leng heard of the Holy Spirit so deeply convicting them of their sins that they made public confession of them, he was very indignant. There had been no such immodest doings in the church in his day as an evangelist, he said.

A group of us, who heard of these remarks, met in earnest prayer. We pleaded especially that the Spirit would convict him of his own sins.

That same day I was the leader for the afternoon session of the Conference. At the close of my address Mr. Leng arose and poured out his heart before God, in confession and contrition. He was pardoned and cleansed and a great peace fell upon his spirit.

For four and a half years he was a blessed witness for Christ. At the end of that time he died suddenly of hemorrhage of the lungs. His excess and his long imprisonment were largely responsible. His dying message was, "Tell Han Ku Niang that I will meet her in Heaven."

Chapter VIII

Chang: Prodigal and Persecuted

L ONG BEFORE the sun was due to gild the tree tops with his golden rays, I turned out of the cold mud hut where I had spent the night, took my seat with my Chinese companion on a rude wheel-barrow en-route to a Conference in the northern section of our territory. Liu Kia Ku was our destination, an equally uninteresting collection of sun-dried mud huts.

We arrived in the evening, weary, cold and hungry, and were seated on the warmest Kang in the house, getting thawed out, when the Chinese Pastors were ushered in. After formal greetings, they said they had been praying during the afternoon, asking for a special guidance for the services, especially for the speaker who should give the opening message that night. "We therefore wasted no time in coming to you, Han Ku Niang, when we heard of your arrival, as we are assured you are chosen to give the message." I almost cried, I felt so ill, tired, and cold. Had I been at home my father would have had me in bed with a trained nurse in attendance.

"Oh it cannot be! It is not so. I am sure. Go back and pray some more. It is positively cruel to ask me. I should be resting and some of you men speaking. You must go back and pray again, before I consent to do this. I have nothing prepared," and much more of like nature.

They left me greatly puzzled, but did as I suggested. They prayed some more, with the same result. Returning a second time they made the same report. I was to deliver the message. By this time I had eaten my supper and felt warmer. With many protestations and much misgiving, I finally agreed.

> **SCRIPTURE TESTIMONY**
>
> *God, with great demonstration of love, forgives the truly repentant*
>
> LUKE 15:11-31

During the day there had been a market in this village. A Chinese farmer named Chang Fang Yuan from a near-by town, doing his business in the market place, happened to engage in conversation with one of the Christians, who invited him to the meeting that evening "to hear a white woman speak Chinese," no mention of the subject to be discussed. My friend Chang promptly said he did not believe a word of what his friend was saying. No woman could speak Chinese so he could understand. Indeed he went so far in the heated argument which followed, as to tell the Christian very plainly, he was a liar, and he, Chang, knew it, and would prove it, as he would spend the night in Liu Kia Ku to attend the service and listen. This he did, with an unlooked for result.

Our place of meeting was a rather commodious tent, erected on a threshing floor near the church. By eight P. M. the tent was packed, men on one side, women on the other, with not an inch of space left for standing room. It must have been at this time that Chang, the farmer, arrived on the scene. He found it impossible to get inside. But being a Chinese man who had made up his mind to hear, he was going to hear. Outside he moved from place to place until, directly behind the rude platform, he discovered one of the flaps open, through which he stuck his head. In this fashion he could both hear and see.

Remember, he had never heard the Good News before. This was the only information he had ever received of the Gospel: the Elders in his home town had sworn an oath and signed it with their blood, that if a foreign missionary or Chinese evangelist would come to their town preaching "The Devil's Doctrine," they would kill them; or if any person or persons in the village would become secondary, or second-class devils (local name for native Christians) they too would be killed without delay.

With this scanty knowledge Chang listened to the story of the Prodigal son and its application to himself. It came a direct revelation of the Holy Spirit enlightening him, uncovering the secret sins of his heart, unveiling the righteousness of God.

The service closed. The crowd dispersed. Chang entered the tent, rapidly made his way to the space before the platform, and flinging himself at my feet he cried out, "I am the prodigal! I am the prodigal! How shall I get back to my Heavenly Father? Will He receive me? Oh, I have wandered so far away! Tell me how to get back?"

We knelt together, pleading for and with him, telling him to say, "Lord, forgive me for Jesus' sake!" Soon the peace of God filled his soul, the Holy Spirit revealing the risen Lord in him. He spent the remaining days of the Conference with us. He had some education and could read.

The parting day came quickly. "My brothers and sisters, pray for me," Chang cried out at one of the closing services. "I may never see you again in the flesh. I go back to die, unless God delivers me."

With heavy hearts we commended him to God and proceeded on our journey.

SCRIPTURE TESTIMONY

Believers will suffer terrible things for the sake of Jesus' name

MATTHEW 24:9-14

Father forgive them, for they know not what they do

LUKE 23:34 · ACTS 7:60

Counted worthy of suffering disgrace for the Name

ACTS 5:41

He returned to his village, his heart overflowing with love to God and man. Like Paul of old, no fear of death could close his mouth or prevent him proclaiming the Good News. He had returned to his Heavenly Father, and his Father had received him.

Down to the market place, into the dense crowd he pushed his way and delivered his message. The crowd rushed on him, furious with hate and anger. Soon a messenger ran into his home crying, "They have killed your husband for preaching the devil's doctrine; he is lying dead in the market place;" and then fled.

Relatives carried the body home, where it was discovered that life was not extinct. One leg was broken in three places, every tooth in the front of his mouth was knocked out of his head, and one eye and one ear were destroyed. Three months he lay on his brick bed unable to move, praying for his enemies and those who had despitefully used him, "Father forgive them, they do not understand," and praising God that he had been found worthy to suffer for Jesus' sake.

Later he prayed for the entire town, asking the Lord to send the Pastors and Miss Vaughan to his benighted village and proclaim the "Good News to all."

A year passed, when the answer came. Every detail was remembered by a loving Heavenly Father. The way opened for me to go and the first two days the Lord gave twenty-five souls, heathen women who had never heard the Word before. The missionary in charge of our station, Dr. Charles Ernest Scott, baptized these women two years later, when I was in America.

The men who had attempted to murder Chang Fang Yuen, when they heard we were coming to hold a Christian Conference in their town, waited on him, saying, "What can we do to help you? Let us dig the holes for the tent poles and put it up. Let us do anything, but let us help."

They attended the meetings and some were converted then and there; all began to attend church and read the scriptures.

Thus grew the body of Christ in China, making increase of itself in love,—a vision of suffering with Christ that the church in the United States has not yet received.

Chapter IX

The Woman Who Saw Heaven

IN THE year of 1904, I held a meeting of several days' duration in the city of Wang Kia Kwan Dswang. My audience consisted of the most stupid and ignorant of Chinese women. Some of them were converts, but most of them came to hear the gospel for the first time. Among these last was a Mrs. Jang, who seemed, if possible, a little more stupid than the rest. She was one of our number not because of any interest she felt in Bible-truth, but because her husband, formerly a Confucian scholar, had accepted the Saviour and wished her to know something of the fundamental principles of Christianity. Her two little children, who were always with her, consumed much of her time and strength. There were some twenty others in the class to be taught and I had little chance to give individual attention. The prospect for her learning enough of the truth to be converted was not encouraging.

SCRIPTURE TESTIMONY
Ask Me anything in My name
MATTHEW 18:19 · JOHN 14:13-14 · JOHN 16:23-24

My one method of work, however, was prayer with complete reliance upon the power of God through the Holy Spirit to fulfill His promise in John 14:13, 14. "And whatsoever ye shall ask in my name, that will I do that the Father may be glorified in the Son. If ye shall ask anything in my name, I will do it." In the course of these meetings the Father was glorified in the conversion of Mrs. Jang; for after four days of simple instruction she returned to her home a new creature in Christ Jesus.

About six months later, when I was holding services in a neighboring village, Mrs. Jang appeared again. This time she brought three children and the family dog. (She had given away the chickens.) Again she stayed four days, absorbed as much truth as she could under the trying circumstances, and again returned home.

Soon after she contracted tuberculosis and suffered intensely for a year. Her physical pain was only a part of her distress. Her family realized that a great change had taken place in her life, but they would not accept her testimony. They were especially bitter because she unbound her feet. Disregarding such a time honored custom was a serious disgrace to them. They tortured her in all sorts of little meannesses. She would be refused a drink when she was too ill to get it for herself, and she was frequently told that she was to be buried with her feet bare. A modest Chinese woman has only her face and hands uncovered, even in death.

In the midst of all her pain and trials Mrs. Jang maintained a bright, clear testimony. She grieved only because her dear ones would not receive the message of life that so thrilled and comforted her own soul.

The dreadful disease had about done its work, when I again found myself in her vicinity. The pastor of the church in which I was speaking came to tell me of her year of suffering.

"Miss Vaughan," he said, "the only prayer she has offered for herself during all these months is that she may see your face again."

Needless to say I went to her immediately. I was received with a welcome of such apparently boundless affection that I felt I had never before known what love was. A few days passed. It was evident that it was God's will to take Mrs. Jang home, and we who loved her ceased to pray for her recovery. We asked only that God would give her great peace in going, and lift from her heart the burden of grief that it carried because her testimony had not been received by those nearest her.

I made what I supposed was my last visit to her. "We will never see our friend on earth again," I said to my class. "She is very near the heavenly home, and can not possibly live through the night."

Early the next morning her father called upon me. "Your daughter is now at rest and in the Saviour's presence," I said.

He smiled. "Oh no, no!" he said excitedly. "The Lord has performed a wonderful miracle. She is alive again!"

Then he explained. Mrs. Jang had died at three o'clock the afternoon before, and her family, in accordance with Chinese custom, had imme-

SCRIPTURE TESTIMONY
God gave a glimpse *of what is to come*
2 CORINTHIANS 12:2

diately prepared her body for burial. At about sunset they heard a noise in the death chamber. They supposed that the children or pigs or chickens (they have equal freedom in the houses of the poor) had gotten into the room. But when they opened the door they could scarcely believe their eyes. Mrs. Jang sat erect on the kang. She had removed her grave clothes and put on those she had been wearing before her death!

I never taught Revelation in China and nothing had ever been told Mrs. Jang of the glories of Heaven as described in that book. She had instruction for only eight days in her life.

This is her story as she related it to me: "I remember seeing all the family around me crying. Then the Lord Jesus came into my room and took me by the hand and said, 'Come with me.' In a short time we were before a gate of pearl. It was the gate of Heaven. Angels opened it and we went in. I saw many beautiful houses all of pretty colors. I walked beside the Lord on the golden streets, and oh, Miss Vaughan, I was so glad you had told me to unbind my feet; I would have been so ashamed to walk beside my Saviour with little feet.

"Then we went on and I saw thousands of angels in a circle, singing and playing lovely music. In the midst was the throne of glory, the Heavenly Father sat upon it and when I saw Him I was afraid. I hardly dared to lift my eyes."

"'You have come,' He said.

"And I answered, 'Yes, Lord.'

"Then He said, 'You may go back for a while, but you must return to me here on the twelfth of the month.'

"So Miss Vaughan, here I am, and now they'll have to accept my testimony, for I have walked on the golden streets and I've seen the Father. They'll have to believe me now."

Did her relatives and neighbors believe her?

People flocked in from miles around to hear the wonderful story. She spoke as an eye witness and they could not reject her testimony. God's mighty power was upon it, and hundreds were converted.

Even today missionaries in that vicinity find an eager reception for the gospel message because that is the "Jesus doctrine" believed by Mrs. Jang who went to heaven and came back again to tell what she saw.

The days passed until the twelfth of the following month. When that day came the family tried to convince Mrs. Jang that she had reckoned the date incorrectly, but her eager heart was not to be deceived. Late in the afternoon she asked her mother for her grave clothes. Under strong protest they were folded and put on the bed. At sunset while the family were at their evening meal in an adjoining room, she dressed herself quietly in her burial garment, then lay down and her beautiful soul went back to her God.

Just an ignorant Chinese woman whose whole education had been gained in a few days; yet how wonderfully God used her to His glory in the saving of souls.

At the coming of our Lord, when every man's work shall be made manifest, shall we who have the light of the glorious gospel from our early youth be able to say with Mrs. Jang, "Father, I have glorified Thee on earth. I have finished the work which Thou gavest me to do."

Chapter X

The Rain Story

THE THEOLOGICAL Seminary of Shan Tung University was located in earlier years in the walled city of Tsing Chao Fu in Shan Tung Province. The cooperating Missions were The English Baptist Mission and the Board of Foreign Missions of the Presbyterian Church, U. S. A.

One of its professors was visiting Tsing Tan in May, 1908, when I returned to my headquarters there. I had been itinerating among the churches for about seven months and I was very tired. This professor very kindly invited me to go to his home for my two weeks of much needed rest. I accepted gladly for I thought the atten-tion and activities of the

SCRIPTURE TESTIMONY
Holy Spirit convicts people of their sin
JOHN 16:8
The prayer of a person in right relationship with God is effective
JAMES 5:16-18
Elijah, a normal human being, prayed for rain
JAMES 5:17

community would be centered in the seminary, and therefore it was not likely that I would be called upon to conduct meetings.

The entire province of Shan Tung (in which I now visited) was suffering from drought, for not one drop of rain had fallen for three months. And while the province has a smaller area than the state of Missouri, its population is twenty-eight and one-half millions. Every one with the exception of the Christians was propitiating the rain god, that is they were offering paper money, food and drink and were having great processions to do him honor.*

The university students were deeply concerned about conditions. They had observed the useless sacrifices of money, food and drink and the numerous processions.

After two days of rest I was surprised to be called upon on Thursday afternoon and asked to hold a half-hour prayer meeting with a few students from my own church territory.

When I entered the class room at the appointed time the twelve Chinese students present stood up and one of them addressed me. "Miss Vaughan, you have been in our homes, and you know everyone of our families. You know what it will mean to us if our wheat crop fails,—famine, pestilence and death.

"Now the whole city with the exception of the Christians, has been praying to the rain-god. We have seen him carried over

---

* The sacred money of China is bought with the currency of the realm, but it has no purchasing value. It is used only as an offering to the gods, or to the spirits of the departed ones at their funerals. Food is presented to the gods and eaten before them. Drink is poured out on the ground in token of dedication to them. Processions also indicate prayer and worship. In those which had been formed every day in Tsing Chao Fu, every family in the city was represented by at least one member,— whenever practicable by the entire household.

the fields day by day for six weeks with the chief official and thousands of the inhabitants of the city following him. Now at last they've given up in despair. They have carried him outside the city walls and cast him in a field. They said to him:—'We leave you here to blister in the sun until you feel some pity for us and our families.'

"We understand why there is no answer to prayers made to this or to any other idol. We are sufficiently educated to know that there is no power in gods of clay. But, Miss Vaughan, we too have been praying for six weeks and God has not answered us. We are face to face with this question, 'Is there anything in this religion of Jesus Christ, or is it, too, just a farce?' We don't know that our God is any more able or willing to answer prayer than the clay rain-god is. We have seen no evidence in this case that He exists at all."

Although these students were honestly doubting the love, the power, and the personality of God they had not wholly lost their faith, 'for they asked,' "Why is it that your prayers and Pastor Ding's are answered and ours not?"

"There are three hindrances to God's answering our prayers," I replied. "Sins of transgression of God's law, sins of non-conformity to His will, and the sin of unbelief. Let me ask you a question. Are you willing to look to God to show you what sins have been hindering your petition for rain, and when He reveals them to you are you willing to confess them?"

"Oh, yes!" they said.

"Then," I answered, "let each of us offer this prayer: Heavenly Father, forgive me my sins, send the Holy Spirit into my heart to reveal them to me. Cleanse me in the precious blood of Jesus and fill me with Thy Holy Spirit for Jesus' sake. Amen.'"

Our knees had scarcely touched the floor before these young
men, some of them unable to finish the little prayer, were sobbing
out a confession of their sins before God; sins of unforgiveness, of
not trusting Him, of hating fellow students; sins of not witnessing for Jesus in their own families; and in the college; sins of
lying, cheating, breaking rules and profaning the Sabbath. Then
we prayed together and asked God to send us the rain.

These young men told their fellow students of what had
occurred and the next day about thirty came to the meeting.
Practically the same questions were asked and the same answers
given. Again we had the outpouring the Spirit in convicting
power. The confessions followed, and again we prayed for rain.

On the third day, Saturday, seventy-five students attended
our meeting, and the experiences of the previous meetings were
repeated.

Then I was invited to lead, at eight o'clock Sunday morning
a prayer meeting of the entire student body, one hundred and
sixty in number.

Once more we had questions and answers similar to those
of our first meeting, we offered our simple prayer and once
more conviction and confession followed. (I was much interested during these days in observing that those students who
attended several of the meetings made further confession of sins
and prayers for cleansing.)

On this Sunday, a committee of students was appointed to wait
upon their professors to ask that all school work be suspended
that the students might devote their time to confession and
prayer. The faculty, delighted with the wonderful manifestation
of God's power, gladly suspended classes for the time, and asked
the committee to arrange for the services they wanted. This was
the daily program:—

7.00-7.30—Prayer for the presence and power of the Holy Spirit throughout the day.

10.00-12.00—Confession of sins and prayer for rain.

1.30-5.00—Students to go, in groups of threes, all over the city explaining to people in the streets, in the stores, workshops, stalls of the market place and even in the residences of the city officials, what was being done among the students.

This was their message, which they had submitted to the faculty for approval: "We have come to you to tell you that we are Christians and that at the Jesus Church we are confessing our sins to the Heavenly Father and asking His forgiveness and praying in the name of His Son Jesus that He will send us rain. Will you join us? You can do so in your own homes or up in the Jesus Church."

The program was adhered to until Thursday night. Still there was no rain. The sky was like brass and the earth like a furnace and full of great cracks because of the dryness. A few more such days and the wheat would be burned up!

On this day I was not in the meetings. The preceding evening the professor who was my host had asked, "Miss Vaughan, how long do you intend to keep this thing up?"

"Just until rain comes," I replied. But realizing that the faith of this man was becoming very weak I resolved to wait upon the Lord in prayer and fasting. About the middle of the morning I opened my Bible to the forty-third chapter of Isaiah. My eyes went straight to the nineteenth verse and my joy was unspeakable as I read that wonderful promise: "Behold I will do a new thing; now it shall spring forth; shall ye not know it? I will even make a way in the wilderness and rivers in the desert."

I closed the book and thanked God for the answer to our prayer.

The next morning we awakened to find the sky covered with black clouds and a light rain falling. The rain continued until three in the afternoon. Then suddenly a strong wind blew the clouds away and the sun shone brighter and hotter than ever. I was resting in my room, when I became aware of people outside the French window, and looking out I saw the entire student body of the Seminary. I soon realized from the urgent questions that were asked that I must give a talk on faith and prayer then and there. That I did.

"Have we sinned so deeply that God is too angry to forgive us?" they asked. "Did He send the rain this morning to show us His power, and did He stop it to teach us that our sins are so great that He cannot give the blessing we ask?"

"No, my brothers," I answered. "'If we confess our sins, He is faithful and just to forgive us our sins and cleanse us from all righteousness.' His love is as boundless as the ocean. His mercy and grace have no limit. There is something more that He wants us to do and we must wait upon Him until He shows us what it is. Let me suggest that instead of going to the city this afternoon (it was already well canvassed) that each of us retire to his own room and that we ask God to reveal to us what He would have us do next."

At the evening meeting one of the students asked permission to speak and came up on the platform. "I know what the will of God is in this matter," he said. "We know what peace and joy we have received by confessing our sins and having them cleansed in the precious blood. The Heavenly Father does not wish us to keep these blessings to ourselves. I propose that tomorrow we again form groups and carry the message, not to the city, but to every one of the twenty-six country churches that belong to this mission.

We can reach the farthest one by tomorrow night, give our message from the pulpit Sunday and return Monday. Who will volunteer?"

In a few minutes more than enough had offered themselves for the service. All arrangements were speedily made, and early the next morning the twenty-six little bands started on their journeys. That same morning we looked up into the sky and saw those wonderful clouds back again and once more a gentle rain fell! By night (when our students had reached their destinations) it was falling heavily, some of the time in perfect torrents. And it continued!—Saturday night and Sunday, Sunday night and Monday—never a respite until Wednesday. Our students returned Monday night, their clothing drenched and their faces shining.

"Oh, Miss Vaughan," they said, "we never knew until now what it means to sing 'Praise God from Whom all blessings flow.'"

And the wheat crop of the entire Province and large neighboring areas was saved!

Again the committee waited upon the faculty of the Seminary. "We have, for ten days, confessed our sins and prayed for rain. God has wonderfully forgiven our sins and answered our prayers. If you, our teachers, made us magnificent presents, we would take time to thank you for them. We have come to ask you to continue the suspension of our classes for ten days more that we may thank the Heavenly Father for forgiving and delivering us and our families from famine and pestilence.

This, their second request, was granted. We had each morning the same half hour for prayer for blessing throughout the day. The forenoons were spent in praise and thanksgiving. In the afternoons the students went throughout the city with another brief message: "We have come to tell that we confessed our sins and prayed to our Heavenly Father for rain. He graciously heard our prayer, and has saved us all from destruction. We are holding praise and thanksgiving services in the Jesus Church. Will you join us? You can do so in your own homes or in the church." This message, like the first, was delivered also at the residence of every official.

All the services began with the doxology,—"Praise God From Whom All Blessings Flow." They consisted of hymns of praise and passages of praise from the Scriptures, of prayers of praise and thanksgiving, and testimonies of praise and thanksgiving for blessings received.

From the first day, citizens from all walks in life flocked to the church. Women hobbled on their poor bound feet from one or two miles in the country round about. Unconverted persons so crowded the church that there was scarcely any space left for the students and Christians. Overflow meetings were held in class-rooms and dormitories.

On the tenth day the chief official with his subordinates and their retinues came to give thanks to God for His deliverance.

He said, "I believe yours is the true God, and that you preach the true gospel. I would become a Christian tomorrow if I did not know that I would lose my place and probably my head."

We hardly know how to go about giving an adequate conception of the results of the abounding spiritual blessings that fell with the great rain on that city and province. They are perhaps more easily imagined by the reader than expressed by the writer.

There was, of course, large increase in attendance at the 'Jesus Church," and transformed lives were observed in all quarters and among all classes of people. It was found that scores had been converted through the testimonies of the beautiful ten days of praise.

In the next chapter we relate a single incident as representative of many that were the outcome of God's gracious answer to our prayer for rain.

Chapter XI

A Sequel to the Rain Story

S O DEEP an impression had been made on the students of the Seminary by God's wonderful answer to the prayer that every one of them asked and received permission to preach in the neighboring villages on Sundays.

The following is but one of the many remarkable occurrences in their ministry:—The strongest anti-foreign and anti-Christian village in the district was near Tsing Chao Fu. Its chief official, who exercised military as well as civil authority, had sworn an oath to take the life of any person who in any way allied himself with Christianity, whether to adopt this "Devil's doctrine" himself or to preach it to others.

SCRIPTURE TESTIMONY
Signs and wonders draw attention to Gospel message
JOHN 4:28-29 · ACTS 8:5-8
Signs and wonders result in mass conversions
ACTS 9:35 · ACTS 9:42

One Sunday, as a group of students passed near the village, a man ran screaming from the village gate, went round and round and dropped apparently lifeless to the ground. A crowd gathered and the students hurried across the field to ascertain the trouble. He was mad, some people told them and others said, "He is possessed by an evil spirit."

"Can't his people care for him?" asked our students.

"He's a stranger in the village," was the reply.

"Well, we are Christians," the students announced bravely, "and we will do what we can to help, and if he has an evil spirit Jesus will cast it out of him." So they took out their Bibles, read a passage of Scripture, and sang a hymn, then knelt in prayer. Then one of the students commanded in Jesus' name that the evil spirit leave the afflicted man. The man sat up, to all appearances perfectly normal. The Christians exhorted him and those standing around him to put their trust in Jesus, and went on their way.

About half a mile from the village men came running after them. "Please, sirs," they begged, "come back to the man, the devil has gone into him again."

They returned and there he lay on the ground again, unconscious as before. A little pile of ashes lay beside him. "Oh, you have been burning incense to the spirit!" the Christians exclaimed. "We told you not to do that and that he would surely return if you worshiped him!"

Oh, no, indeed, they had done nothing of the kind, they said. But when they saw that the Christians were angry and were going to leave them alone with the man they thought to be dying, they fell upon their knees, confessed that they had burned incense and begged the students to drive the demon away once more. And all this, not out of pity for the dying man but because the Chinaman believes he will be haunted by the spirits, good and bad, of anyone who dies on his property. So the students offered a prayer for the deliverance of the afflicted one and again the evil spirit left him.

The villagers' delight knew no bounds, for aside from their relief, they were deeply impressed by the power manifest in this belief and they all but worshiped the Christians.

"Won't you come into the village and tell us more of this Jesus doctrine?" they begged.

What an opportunity! Here were the Christians who would not have dared to enter that bitterly anti-Christian village a few hours before, being invited, even begged by a crowd of the villagers themselves, to come in and preach the gospel. They were only too glad to say yes. The following Monday they returned, held meetings for three days, entirely unmolested, and sixty people in that one small village were intelligently converted.

Chapter XII

The Demoniac

A N INCIDENT that occurred during the course of my life in China awakened me to a realization of the sin of unbelief in my own life and in the hearts of other Christian workers. Although I had left my family, my home and my country for my Master's sake and at His call, I was made to see that, in spite of all this, I was grieving Him by not trusting His word more fully.

During a morning session of one of my classes of Chinese women, the most pitiful creature I have ever seen was brought to me by her father and brother. Wild eyes, matted hair, tattered clothing, and a skin covered with sores, made her look more like a captured animal than a human being. The poor little

SCRIPTURE TESTIMONY
Demons cast out in Jesus' name
MATTHEW 8:16-17 · MATTHEW 8:28-32 · MATTHEW 9:32-34 · MARK 1:23-26 · MARK 9:20-27 · LUKE 10:17
God using an inner voice to communicate
ACTS 10:19-20 · ACTS 11:12

baby with her was no less pitiful and its body, too, was covered with sore places. The woman had made those places, the father told me, by pinching out little pieces of her own flesh and her baby's.

All this misery had been brought on by the cruelty of an idol-worshiping husband and mother-in-law, for, although the woman was unconverted herself, she came from a Christian family.

I was appalled. The poor creature was evidently ill as well as deranged. We were far from a physician and over four thousand miles from the only hospital for the insane, at that time, in all China.

In my perplexity and hardly realizing what I was doing, I asked my class how many of them would join me in prayer, believing God could and would help her. There were six Bible women present and to my astonishment every one of them stood up.

I now realized that I had committed myself to trusting the Lord, and though I felt no direct assurance that He would hear me in this case, to draw back was to put a limit on His love and power. So boldly, I claimed . the promise in John 14: 13-14. "And whatsoever ye shall ask in My Name that will I do that the Father may be glorified in the Son. If ye shall ask anything in My Name I will do it."

During the next few days we prayed frequently about this matter and during that same time the women of my class came to me again and again to tell me that the woman was possessed of an evil spirit.

"That is not so," I told them very positively. "In Christ's day there was demon possession, but learned men today tell us that no such thing exists in this century."

I had accepted the word of scientists and not my Bible, and because of that unbelief in my heart, I hindered God's mercy and power for that woman for more than a week.

For seven days we had prayed and her condition was no better. Then on the eighth day, as I was seated ready to eat my breakfast, the Lord spoke to me, saying, "This kind goeth not out but by prayer and fasting" (Matthew 18: 21). I was willing to fast and began to do so immediately.

A few minutes later two of the Bible women came to tell me that the Lord had commanded them to fast and to ask me if I would join them. While we were still speaking, two more came from another quarter of the village with exactly the same request. The five of us stood marveling at the wonderful manifestation of God's will when, looking up, we saw the other two coming towards us. We knew before they told their message that it was a repetition of the others.

So we fasted, and prayed for the woman as before. At noon I had her brought to me. I was determined that she should confess her sins, and ask God to heal her disease or insanity as I, in my persistent belief, chose to call it. I told her to repeat after me these words:—"Heavenly Father, forgive me my sins and heal me in Jesus' name."

She followed me obediently until she came to the word "Jesus." "I will not say that name, I will not!" she screamed, and, tearing out her hair by the roots, she threw it on the floor and spat upon it.

"You shall say that name," I said and pressed her down to her knees again. For an hour I continued to push her down whenever she attempted to rise and command her to say "In Jesus' name." And at last she obeyed.

She was much calmer after that, but she was far from being a sane woman.

But I had learned my lesson and by five o'clock in the afternoon I was ready to open up the channel of God's power by accepting His written word as true.

Walking into the room where the woman was, I went up to her and said, "In Jesus' name, I command thee, thou evil spirit, to leave this woman and never return."

Catching up her child she rushed from the room and to her home, two of the Bible women after her. In her home she fell upon her bed, violently ill, and remained so for twenty-four hours. After this she fell into a long, quiet sleep, from which she awoke a perfectly sane woman.

She came to my class, learned two pages of her catechism, gained a knowledge of prayer, and, best of all, accepted Jesus 'Christ as her personal Saviour.

Chapter XIII

The Adopted Sons

T HE FIRST work I ever did in any of Pastor Chao's churches
was in response to an invitation to teach a class of fifty-six
women in Da Shin Tan, Shan Tung Province.

Among these women was a Mrs. Liu, a Christian widow
whose husband had died about ten years before; and he, in
his provision for her, had adopted two nephews as his sons
and heirs. To them he had bequeathed fifty acres of land and
some money with the understanding that they were to care
for their aunt. To her he left a smaller sum of money, ten acres
and a house.

These men misused their fortune and became gamblers and
opium smokers. They mortgaged their property heavily and were
soon reduced to poverty. Covetousness and dishonesty filled
their hearts and under their management of the aunt's little farm
much of the produce disappeared. She remonstrated, of course,
and the first ten years of her widowhood was a series of quarrels.

Seven weeks previous to my visit in Da Shin Tan, these
bickerings had culminated in an attempt to take the life of the

aunt. Her nephews had beaten her with a heavy bamboo pole, such as the Chinese use for carrying water, and left her dead, as they supposed, on the floor of her home.

In the middle of the night she had regained consciousness. She .was frightfully bruised and cut and could not walk, but she dared not remain in the house, so she had dragged herself on hands and knees to a neighbor's house. There she hid until she was able to escape to the church at Da Shin Tan.

Her nephews returned and stole her money, bedding, grain, and even the cheap straw mat on her kang. Worst of all, they had helped themselves to the deed to her property.

Pastor Chao and Elder Ding were deeply concerned when they heard this story and immediately set about doing everything they could to help her. Their efforts were in vain, however, for the nephews denied all knowledge of the crime.

"Who beat our aunt and stole her things?" they asked innocently. "We don't understand what she is doing in Da Shin Tan village. Tell her to come right home."

The day I arrived in the village I was told the story and requested to do what I could to help.

"What plans has the church in mind ?" I asked Elder Ding and Pastor Chao.

"Well, we have two plans!" they told me." One is to arrange for this woman to marry again, then her husband could protect her."

An ideal Chinese plan, I thought to myself, for marriage is the way out of most any difficulty in which the Chinese woman happens to find herself.

"And why don't you carry out this plan ?" I asked the gentlemen.

"We are waiting for you to help us."

"And how can I help?" I inquired.

They hesitated and blundered and finally I had it,—the woman didn't want a second husband. In fact, she had wept incessantly since he had been mentioned to her.

I gave them to understand that I would never do the least thing to force this woman into an unwelcome marriage.

"Now," I said, "let's have your second plan."

The second plan was that they proceed to law.

"Why don't you go ahead with your law-suit?" I demanded.

"We can't without your help. You know, Miss Vaughan, that to get a hearing with any official, you must make him a present of a large sum of money. Mrs. Liu's money is all gone. We can't mortgage her property with the deed gone, too. Now, you are a member of the great American Mission, can't you just write a letter to the official and ask for justice for her?"

I explained that only one member of our mission had this privilege. I could ask him to write such a letter but it would be a month before we could get a reply.

"All right, that settles the matter," they concluded. "There's nothing more to be done."

"But, my brothers," I said, "you haven't asked me for my plan."

"Have you a plan!"

"Oh, yes, mine isn't anything like yours, but I can guarantee it to work."

They were astounded and incredulous. My next remark left them resentful.

"I shall not tell you my plan," I said, "until you promise to adopt it."

For quite a few minutes such a suggestion seemed preposterous to them, but finally curiosity got the upper hand and they promised. Then I said, "God says in the Old Testament, Exodus 22: 22-24, 'Ye shall not afflict any widow, or fatherless child. If those afflict them in any wise, and they cry at all unto Me, I will surely hear their cry. And My wrath shall wax hot, and I will kill you with the sword; and your wives shall be widows, and your children fatherless.' The Lord has also given us unlimited latitude in John 14: 13-14. 'And whatsoever ye shall ask in My name, that will I do that the Father may be glorified in the Son. If ye shall ask anything in My name I will do it.' My plan is to ask God to just undertake this whole task for us. And when we have made our petition we will wait until God answers it."

My Chinese brethren were quite sure I was insane, but they had promised and they were helpless. Later we knelt and prayed very simply, asking God to forgive our sins and the sins of Mrs. Liu and her nephews and undertake this matter.

This occurred on Wednesday and as often as we had opportunity from that day until Sunday, we waited upon God with our petition. Sunday morning Pastor Chao came running after me as I left the church.

"Read that, read that!" he demanded, thrusting a foot and a half of Chinese letter into my hands. "It is just wonderful,—just wonderful! The Lord has answered our prayer." He gave me no time to read the letter, but hurried to tell me the contents himself. "It says four peace-makers are coming tomorrow to settle Mrs. Liu's affairs."

"I knew that God would do this thing so much better than we possibly could," I said.

"Oh, I know you said that, Miss Vaughan, but I didn't know it would be like this—this is wonderful!"

The entire church was deeply impressed.

Early Monday morning the four peace-makers (lawyers) arrived, and I was asked to meet them. Now, it is the custom for peace-makers representing both sides to meet, and, after haggling for hours, sometimes days, to settle on a more or less satisfactory compromise. Knowing this and desiring to be concerned in no affair which could dim the glory due to God I sent word to the peace-makers (much to the chagrin of Pastor Chao) that I would not consent to talk to them unless they were ready to assure me that the last stick and thread of Mrs. Liu's property would be restored to her at once.

Pastor Chao came running back from them immediately. "Why, Miss Vaughan, this is the most wonderful of all, they say that is just what they came to do!"

On Tuesday the officers of the church saw every bit of Mrs. Liu's property restored to its proper place, received from the nephews the key and a written promise to treat their aunt with all respect in the future and returned to the village in triumph.

On Wednesday, just one week from the day on which we offered our first prayer, Mrs. Liu's nephews knelt and asked her forgiveness, asked me to pray for them, and led their aunt back to her home. From that day to the day of my departure for America there was not only a complete absence of strife in that family, but many people in the vicinity became Christians because of the testimony of Mrs. Liu and her nephews.

For about six months after the reunion of the Lius I prayed from time to time that God would in some way let me know what means He had used to effect such a complete change in those two men. I wanted all the facts that bore on this manifestation of "the greatness of His power to us-ward who are believing."

At the end of this time my Chinese servant went for a visit to the home of his people in a village about two miles from the home of Mrs. Liu.

On his return he rushed into my study, crying, "Oh, Miss Vaughan, the Lord performed a miracle for Mrs. Liu! Don't you remember the woman we prayed for in the spring-time ?" I was secretly amused at the "we", for this same boy had' considered mere praying and "doing nothing" a poor way out of the difficulty. But I kept a straight face and asked him to tell me about it.

SCRIPTURE TESTIMONY
God communicating in a dream
MATTHEW 1:20 · MATTHEW 27:19 · ACTS 2:17

"Why," he said, "all the people in her village and mine are talking about it. You remember that letter came Sunday morning. Well, in the middle of the Saturday night one of the nephews awoke screaming with fright and crying out that he was going to be killed. When the people in the house could get him quieted sufficiently, he told them that a man had come and stood beside him while he slept. 'I am the Lord Jesus Whom your aunt worships,' He said. 'You must never beat her again and you must restore her property. If you will do this at once, go to a foreign woman named Han Ku Niang (Miss Louisa Vaughan) at Da Shin Tan, and she will make it right for you and you will suffer no harm. But if you delay I shall slay you with this sword in My hand.'"

The household was alarmed and when the other nephew told them of exactly the same experience their alarm turned to terror. Before morning four peacemakers sat at a feast and received explanation and instruction as to what must be done, and at the suggestion of the peace-makers the letter was written which announced the settlement of affairs early Monday morning. The rest of the story you know.

Many good Christians believe that they must help the Lord,— that their talents are to be used in His service in just that way. My own experience in this case and in many others is contrary to this view, and in accordance with the Lord's teaching in John

6: 28-29—"Then said they unto Him, 'What shall we do that we might work the works of God?' Jesus answered and said unto them, 'This is the work of God, that ye believe on Him Whom He hath sent!'"

My experience in my life of faith has been a verification of Ephesians 1: 18-20. "The eyes of your understanding being enlightened, that ye may know what is the hope of His calling, and what the riches of the glory of His inheritance in the saints, and what is the exceeding greatness of His power to us-ward who believe, according to the working of His mighty power which He wrought in Christ when He raised Him from the dead and set Him at His own right hand in the heavenly places."

Chapter XIV

A Chinese Law Suit

URING THE years of my service for Christ in Shantung
Province, I was brought into frequent contact with Pastor
Chao, a dear old saint of God. It was my privilege to be
closely associated with him during the weeks of stress and strain
which followed the persecution of the church of Kwoa Kia Tai Tsz.

The Chinese heart, regenerated by Christ, is merciful and
tender; but in none of the three great religions of China are
there found the principles expressed in such passages as, "Love
your enemies, do good to them that hate you," and "Father,
forgive them for they know not what they do." The unconverted
Chinese never forget wrongs, are bitterly unforgiving, and miss
no opportunity for revenge.

The official who conducts a Chinese law-suit seldom makes
a pretense of doing so on a basis of justice; in fact he is very
likely to decide the case in favor of the party who offers the
largest gift. Yet in spite of such conditions, law-suits abound in
China. A family or community, entirely free from legal contro-
versy, is rarely found.

It had occurred, however, that an unconverted Chinese judge had rendered a decision against an idol-worshiper and in favor of a Christian, an elder in Pastor Chao's church at Kwoa Kai Tai Tsz. The persecution referred to above was the result of the resentment in the heart of the elder's opponent.

Some time after the law-suit certain citizens invited their Christian neighbors to confer with them in regard to a site for a new temple to their earth-god. To this little god, whose temple is seldom more than twenty feet square, all deaths are reported. A spot directly in front of the church seemed to be the choice for a site, and, of course, the Christians objected.

But before any location could be decided upon a relative of those in charge of building the temple died, and the temple was erected for the important ceremony of reporting a death, with no more discussion.

A little later some Christian children discovered the little idol in its little temple almost in the church door. They had been taught to hate idols and, moreover, they were deeply offended to find an idol in such a place, so they carried it off and threw it into the river.

At that the storm broke. On Sunday morning, while the Christians were at worship, sixty men burst in upon them, smashing windows, doors and furniture. Those Christians who were unable to escape were beaten and two of them lay in a very serious condition for more than five weeks. Next they raided the houses of church members in the vicinity, destroying furniture, food and fuel. The elder and a good deacon were bound and carried off to the nearest magistrate. To him one rioter displayed a wound in his arm and, handing over a gun belonging to the elder, swore that he had been shot while he and his friends had been peaceably remonstrating over the case of the earth-god.

The two Christians protested that these things were not true; but they were not believed and were cast into prison to await trial.

Meanwhile, the members of Pastor Chao's three churches, stirred deeply by the whole outrageous affair, demanded justice as subjects of the empire.

Mr. —, the missionary in charge of all our work, was besieged by church officers, who with Pastor Chao urged him to intercede in behalf of the men in prison, of the Christians who had been beaten, and for the restoration of church and personal property that had been destroyed.

Mr. D— refused to grant their request, for, as he said, he was not sure where the original fault was. The Christians were irritated and in the meantime two men were in prison and two others were desperately ill.

However, Mr. D— did call for intercessory prayer, and, claiming the promise in John 14: 13-14, we took all the difficulties to the Lord. We asked that God would forgive

> **SCRIPTURE TESTIMONY**
>
> *Ask Me anything in My name*
>
> MATTHEW 18:19 · JOHN 14:13-14 · JOHN 16:23-24

the Christians if they were at fault and that He would protect them if they were innocent. Day after day we prayed, for forty-two days, and day after day things looked darker for the Christians and brighter for the idol-worshipers.

The strongest evidence against the prisoners was the gun. The deacon swore that it belonged to the elder and the elder frankly admitted it. His denial would have meant nothing, for the gun bore his name in full. The prisoners told exactly the same story, namely that a rioter entering the church had shot at the elder, who dodged under a table, and that the rioter who accused the elder had caught the bullet in his arm as he raised his hand to strike a Christian woman on the head. No one believed the story.

But we had asked the Lord to bring the truth to light and He had not forgotten our prayer. On the afternoon before the sentence was to be pronounced, the official was moved by a strange impulse to take to pieces the elder's gun. Strange, I say, because a Chinese gentleman never does anything himself which can be delegated to a servant. The gun was thoroughly clogged with dust and dirt! It could not possibly have been fired in years.

The official immediately sent for the elder and the deacon, showed them the gun and gave them their freedom. He would see to it that they won their case, he said, if they would bring a counter-suit against their accusers.

When the two men reported their deliverance there was great rejoicing. In the midst of a praise meeting in the church the leaders of the persecution appeared, and, prostrating themselves on the floor, begged for mercy. "We will restore your property," they promised, "and pay any sum of money you suggest if only you will not bring suit against us before that official."

To the honor of God, these church members freely forgave them and asked only that the lost property be restored and that the expense incurred for treatment for the sick be defrayed.

And thus the whole community, Christian and unconverted, was brought to the knowledge that our Heavenly Father is a God of power, and One that hears and answers prayer.

Chapter XV

My Cook's Transformation

FOR THE second time in my life in China I was considering the problem of getting a cook. This might seem a very easy matter to the uninitiated, who only consider the population (thirty-eight and one-half millions, in a province the same size as the State of Mississippi). But quality is what you want in a Chinese cook—not quantity.

In my helplessness I betook myself to prayer. My petition was that my Lord would send me the man He desired me to have. It is likely if I had prayed, "Please, dear Lord, send me just such another man as I have had, efficient, reliable, honest, and a Christian," I might have had my prayer answered exactly as I requested. If it had occurred to me to remember that my Father in Heaven had sent His Son to die for the lost, I might have saved myself quite a little anxiety, but I did not. I needed a cook, so I prayed for one. Days passed. The only candidate for the position was my neighbor's boy, a young man with an awful reputation. Of course, a missionary could not possibly employ a man of that kind. Mr. Hwoa, the Chinese teacher, turned him down once, twice, three times. During all these days I wondered why my prayer was not answered.

One day I stepped into my study and waiting for me was a brisk-looking young Chinese man. He soon told me his business—a cook desiring to work for me. Lived next door! To my horror it was the same individual back again. Resolutely determined to put a stop to his hopes once and forever, I inquired if he knew the reputation he bore, reciting for his benefit the list of sins I had heard he was guilty of—lying, drinking, stealing, gambling, etc.

> **SCRIPTURE TESTIMONY**
>
> *True disciples forsake the old self and put on the new self*
>
> EPHESIANS 4:20-27 ·
> EPHESIANS 4:28-5:9 · EPHESIANS
> 5:10-20 · COLOSSIANS 3:5-17

He patiently listened until I finished, and then in a gentle voice said, "Well, didn't you come to my country to teach us to be good?" Completely non-plussed, I could find no words to reply. After a lengthy pause, I said: "I was not aware you wanted to learn to be good."

"Oh, yes, that is exactly what I want," he said, "someone to teach me to be good. I heard you taught the Chinese women, so I came to you to learn."

Still fearful of some hidden desire to work evil upon me, I discouraged him in every way. "Have you ever tried to be good? It is not so easy as you seem to imagine," I suggested, and other remarks of a like nature, but nothing discouraged him. I realized there was no escape. He was determined to learn to be good and from me! Well, I thought, I shall put the bars up so high he cannot hold out, and in that way I shall be through with him in a few days.

Addressing him aloud, I said: "Well, I shall give you one chance. Now, understand, just one chance. If I find you once, only once, drinking, gambling, lying, or going to the market without my permission, then you must leave my house, never to return. Many times since I have thought of myself in connection with this boy of eighteen. Suppose the Lord had given me only one chance, I, who had failed again and again. Wang Si Fu—that was his name—agreed to my conditions.

Perhaps readers in America will not understand why I only gave him one chance. This is because they do not and cannot understand the perils which beset the missionaries working amongst the Chinese women. Amongst mission workers it required the mighty grace of a mighty Lord to enable me to give this man this one chance.

On his arrival on the next day I immediately began to pray for his conversion, which occurred in less than a week. We were at morning prayers. I had taught him in the meantime to pray, "Heavenly Father, forgive me my sins. Cleanse me from them in the precious blood of Jesus. Fill me with Thy Holy Spirit. In Jesus' Name." God abundantly answered that prayer, beyond all I could ask or think.

Utterly illiterate when he came to me, in a year's time he was able to read and write and keep accounts. One day he told me his family history. The eldest boy in a family of three, his home was in a little village in a peaceful valley, where he had never heard of white folks or their Bible. Well-to-do, according to Chinese ideals, he was betrothed to a girl six years his senior when he was a baby of two. Married at fourteen, his wife twenty, he began to assume authority at fifteen, which she deeply resented. Dealing with her in strict conformity with Chinese ethics, he administered a severe beating with a stick. She in revenge promptly threw herself into a well and was drowned. Her family, to secure all the money possible, instituted a law suit, and he had to pay "two thousand cash" (the enormous sum of one dollar in United States money).

The rank injustice of this was too much for human endurance, so he bundled up his little store of clothing and money in a large piece of colored muslin, shook the dust of his native village from the soles of his feet, came to Tsing Tau, and there was hired by one of the non-commissioned officers on a German battleship, and in due time became the captain's boy. What vice and evil he had escaped learning in a heathen village he became proficient in on this vessel. After three years, tired of seafaring life, he came ashore, found a position as cook in the German family who lived next door to me.

When I heard his tale I sent him home to beg his parents' forgiveness for his lack of filial duty. The village was distant four miles from Tsing Tau. About two hundred people lived there and they were all sur-named "Wang." Every person in the village was a relative, far off or near, of my cook.

His announcement to his family and village was: "I have learned to be good and have returned to give you an opportunity to see for yourselves a changed man." Wonder, consternation and quite a percentage of criticism prevailed when he declared that being good involved leaving the spirits of his ancestors to their own devices, giving them neither worship nor offerings, turning away from idols and accepting God's Son, Jesus Christ, as his Saviour. This Saviour, being God's Son, was able to save him in this world from sin and Satan, and afterwards give him a mansion in Heaven. There was nothing to say. Every mouth was closed, every tongue was dumb. He was good. No more gambling, no more drinking, and his wages saved and brought home to his mother, a positive proof that he was a changed man. Wang Si Fu was a new creature in Christ Jesus.

After his second visit there could be no further doubt. He was a good man, a new creation forth from the hand of God, a miracle of love and grace. All could see. Blessed simplicity of God's plan. Would that it were used more in this country.

SCRIPTURE TESTIMONY
Unbelievers pleading to hear the Gospel
ACTS 16:9-10

In a few weeks I received a long letter written in Chinese, signed by the village elders, three of them over ninety years of age, Wang's great-grandfather and two great-granduncles. Would I be kind enough, they wrote, to visit their village and preach this new doctrine, which could make men good. I wrote in reply, telling them it was neither Chinese nor Western etiquette for a woman teacher to preach, but I would send the evangelist in a few days to teach them. In less than a week Mr. Hwoa, the native evangelist, visited their village. They entertained him in a kindly, liberal fashion, but never once invited him to preach. Returning, he informed me that they were nothing but a lot of hypocrites; they had no intention of learning the doctrine, or becoming Christians; they did not wish to listen. I thought it very strange, but said nothing, accepting his report without question. A few weeks later another letter arrived with the same request: "Would I be gracious enough to visit their unworthy village and teach them this new doctrine?" I again refused, but suggested Mr. S., a fellow missionary, as an excellent substitute. A third letter came, saying very plainly, "We have no doubt Mr. S. is all you say, but up till this time we have not had opportunity to see his work. We have seen yours, so please come over and help us. We desire to learn from you. Oh, come and teach us. We are hungry to learn." These people were heathen, so did not understand it was the Lord's work they had seen.

Needless to say, I finally went, taking Wang Si Fu along. Three Chinese women who loved the Lord accompanied us. Four days were spent going to and from this village. Today there is a large group of Christians here who gather for worship in Wang's home.

My adopted son, as Wang liked to call himself, would not cook for any other missionary. After he found out I was not returning to China he wrote me to say he had gone home and was in some small business, where he had freedom to preach Jesus, whom he loved.

Chapter XVI

The Pirate Island

AFTER TEACHING equirers' classes for six or seven years in the organized Chinese churches, scattered over Southeast Shan Tung, Dr. C of Chefoo, invited me to extend my spring trip further north and help a group of women he was greatly interested in.

This journey led me through the beautiful Lao Mountains, whose rocky peaks rise almost out of the sea. Beautiful hidden bays and charming little creeks are formed along the coast by this mountain range, making admirable lurking places for number-less pirates, who ply their dreadful and deadly trade up and down the entire length of China's coast.

The village I was traveling towards, Wang Tsen Tao, together with almost a score of villages and towns, had formerly been on an island. During the course of a few years a remarkable natural phenomenon had taken place, causing the coast on either side to rise, and the island when I visited it was joined to the mainland by a long level strip of sand over which ran the high road.

The island was very attractive, a range of low hills rising near the center, its highest peak being over one thousand feet. This peak was called by the Chinese "Yellow Mountain." Half way up nestled a Buddhist Temple, which added a touch of life to the scene, making an entrancing picture.

I was charmed, promising myself some delightful excursions in the form of pleasant strolls up the delightful shady sides of the mountain, perchance the view from the summit.

A few days later, realizing the need of fresh air and exercise, I stepped out of the Church Courtyard into the village street, passed by the threshing floors, where the peasants were still busy winnowing out the freshly threshed grain. The evening was perfect and I walked rapidly along the road leading directly up the hill, enjoying the exquisite scenery and fresh air. Suddenly voices seemed to be loudly calling my name from behind. At first I paid no attention, thinking I must be mistaken. Slacking my pace, however, I was not left long in doubt. Very distinctly a number of people were running after me, screaming at the top of their voices, "Han Ku Niang, stop!" It did not occur to me to fear. I knew my Lord was with me as he had promised, "Lo, I am with thee all the days." But my curiosity was aroused.

Turning to meet the men, I said, "What's the matter with you people?"

"Oh, Han Ku Niang," the foremost cried, "Why did you walk this way alone?" Why did you not say where you were going; we would then have warned you. Come back, quickly, before the priests see us on this road. If they catch as much as a glimpse of us we shall all be killed. This is their roadway to the sea.

I returned quietly with them, as I could see they were frightened out of their wits. Arrived at the church, I enquired fully their reasons for so great alarm.

"We knew you didn't understand," they said, "The priests in the Yellow Temple are not priests except in name. They are pirates! While half of their number stay in the temple on guard, the others patrol the coast, and woe betide the ill-fated vessels which fall into their hands."

At this point of the conversation, the church doors were carefully closed, and voices lowered so no one on the outside could hear a whisper.

"The pirates mode of procedure is to kill every person on board the doomed ship, rob the bodies of all money and valuables and then cast them into the sea. The human beings disposed of, the rest is simple, namely, to transfer everything of value from the captured vessel to their own; bore a hole in the keel and sink it, without a trace.

"The booty is brought ashore during the night. And do you see that little house on the beach? The loot is placed there, and later conveyed by that very road you were so carelessly walking on and placed in a cave underneath the temple, where piles of gold, silver, precious stones and jewelry of all kinds, priceless pieces of embroidery, valuable bales of silk are stored away, the unlawful loot of the pirates.

"Strange to say, all who travel by that mountain road, disappear at the deep ravine you were nearing, and are never seen again. Are you surprised that we made haste to recall you?"

Very gratefully I thanked the Christians for their loving intervention, ere I fell into the trap of the Buddhists of the Yellow Temple.

It was to this very island the Imperial German Government in 1911 sent a Gun-Boat with a large body of Marines, who landed near this spot, and for days and weeks together, besieged the pirates' stronghold. Over fifty German soldiers were killed, others wounded. The expedition was compelled to retreat, its mission unfulfilled. The soldiers failed to capture the pirates and destroy this awful traffic. I have not heard whether the Japanese Government which in 1914 forcibly took this territory from Germany, and hold it now, have been any more successful in their efforts to stamp out this trade.

It was in this village, "Wang Tsu Tao," that I ran off with a full-grown woman. She, poor thing, had heard the gospel, believed and received the Lord as her personal Saviour. After her baptism her father and mother-in-law were greatly outraged by her defiance of Chinese age-long custom, in unbinding her tiny feet. They beat and threatened her with death, if she continued to disgrace their family by this conduct. She came to me pleading for help, and, as was my custom, I took the matter to the Lord in prayer.

Several days passed. When I had leisure, I journeyed to the village where her family lived, requesting to see her father-in-law. I asked that his daughter- in-law be permitted to accompany me to Tsing Tao, there to look for her husband, and find out his opinion regarding this matter. For some unknown reason, the father-in-law agreed. Then and there, I told the woman quickly to get on my wheel-barrow, and have the men proceed at once on our homeward journey. "I shall overtake you a few minutes later," I said.

Then stepping out of the courtyard into the street, I came face to face with the angry mother-in-law.

"Where are you taking my daughter to?" she demanded in a loud voice, while a crowd of angry relatives gathered around.

"To Tsing Tao to find her husband," I replied. Carefully edging along the wall with my back to it, so no one could get behind me, at the same time keeping an eye on die wheel-barrow, slowly making its way along the up-hill road.

Knowing how few Chinese men know how to run, I kept creeping along by the wall, and talking rapidly at the same time, explaining to them that when I discovered the woman's husband, I would send her home again. At last I arrived at the end of the wall, with the crowd increasing every moment, at the same time becoming more and more incensed. Then amidst a gentle shower of stones and pieces of clay, I quickly picked up my skirts and ran as I never ran before or since in my life. The crowd was petrified with astonishment, seeing a woman run. They did not even attempt to follow me. In a few moments I overtook the wheel-barrow, mounted, and escaped safely with my woman.

Home again, I found her husband an inmate of a German prison in Tsing Tao. Later evidence was produced showing that he had not legally married her, but instead had given her a paper with a few Chinese characters written on it. In this document, he promised to bury her father's body in their family burying ground, for which she was to pay him two hundred Mexican dollars. Then handing her the paper, he told her it was as good as a marriage certificate. Under these circumstances, I constituted myself her guardian.

In the fifteen schools under my care at this time, I had none which she could attend. She was quite untrained, utterly illiterate, and totally unfit to earn her own living. I requested the Christians to pray with me, and ask the Lord to give us a school where she and other Christian women who were dependent could be trained to support themselves. We had only one pupil when we began our prayer circle. This was Mrs. Sung. We needed other pupils, a building, a teacher, and funds to support the school.

Twelve months passed. In the meantime, the Lord had provided all we desired. A Chinese building with fourteen rooms for the school, a matron, a teacher, and eleven other pupils, and the necessary funds as they were required.*

I was privileged to see these women trained and sent out as Bible women and kindergarten teachers, most of them doing effective work in the Master's vineyard, before I left China. Today, so far as I know, those who are still alive, are still witnessing for Him whom they love, because He first loved them.

---

* This is the Women's Bible Training School referred to in Chapter I.

Chapter XVII

The Graves of the Gods

I N THE spring of 1911 a little group of Chinese Christians dwelling in Lao Shan Wei, stirred by the reports of revivals in various

SCRIPTURE TESTIMONY

All great movements of God are birthed in prayer

ACTS 1:14

churches in Chimo County, began to intercede with God for their community. They asked Him for a conference in their midst, to which He would send leaders who had been the means of blessing in these other places. They prayed for a whole year, all the while waiting patiently and expectantly for the answer.

At the end of this time they saw that God was working, for the speakers they had chosen had all consented to come (I was one of them) and their non-Christian neighbors had begun to manifest most remarkable interest in the proposed meetings.

But a great difficulty still remained in the way. The hall owned by the Christians of the town was the only one in which the gospel had been preached, and this was far too small to accommodate the unconverted friends who had already expressed a desire to attend the services.

Those who understand conditions in China, and have some conception of the bitter prejudice of the unconverted against Christians, know that it was only by the direct power of God that an audience room could possibly be secured.

The Christians made their need of a hall a special subject of prayer and asked God to give them one large enough to hold the people He was going to send.

In due time my six Bible women and I found ourselves on the way to meet our engagement at Lao Shan Wei. We could travel only twenty miles of the distance by rail. The remaining forty had to be covered in wheel barrows.

A Chinese wheel barrow is one large wheel with boards for seats on each side. There are handles at the back, which the coolie holds, and a rope drawn across his shoulders and fastened to the handles helps him to balance his load. A coolie gives his services and the use of the barrow and donkey for about two dollars a day. Out of this sum he provides food for himself and his donkey.

In all my fifteen years in China I never became expert or even fairly graceful in mounting and leaving wheel barrows. I either rose too quickly and precipitated my companion in the dust, or else I was too slow and was tumbled to the ground myself, in a most undignified manner.

For two days we jolted along in our barrows and reached Lao Shan Wei at about dusk. We were tired and travel-stained, and we little dreamed that for six hours bright eyes had strained for a glimpse of our quaint little caravan. But that was just the case, for a crowd of boys from the Christian school of the place had been sitting on the wall since noon waiting to welcome us. As we drew near the city they rushed out the South gate to meet us. They were most delighted to see me, for I was the first white woman they had ever laid eyes upon. When I had alighted from my barrow they clutched my hands and skirts and pulled me under the archway of the gate.

"Come along fast!" they urged. "Do come along fast and see where the gods are buried!" In the court yard of a temple they threw their caps into the air and danced over some newly-turned clay.

What was it all about! I called a man standing near by and asked him if he could explain

SCRIPTURE TESTIMONY
God leads believers in opposition to idolatry
ACTS 17:16-17 · I CORINTHIANS 8:4 · I JOHN 5:21
God answers prayer
LUKE 18:7 · JOHN 15:7 · ACTS 12:5 · JAMES 5:15

what the children meant. He was a Christian and was only too glad to tell me the story:—

"A month ago while we were still praying for a hall for our Conference, I happened to meet the chief official of our city on the street. I told him of the Christian meetings we were to hold and timidly asked if it would be possible for us to use one of the government buildings for just a few days. He led me to this temple and asked me if it would do. He told me to look it over and tell him what I thought.

"'Your Excellency,' I answered, 'the temple is ample in size for our purpose, but it is already occupied.'

"'Occupied,' said the official, 'what do you mean?'

"'Why just this,' I answered. 'Such a large part of the temple is filled with idols that the part which remains would accommodate no more people than our own little hall.'

"'Oh, is that all ?' he replied. What he said next set me trembling from head to foot. 'Just go down and throw those idols out, they are of no use.'

"'Oh, your Excellency,' I gasped. 'The people!— why they would tear us to pieces instead of coming to our meetings!'

"'I don't believe they would,' he said. 'A few years ago we knew no better than to worship them, but now we know they are useless. I'll assume the responsibility at any rate, so you just do as I say, and I'll see that no one molests you.'"

"Wondering at God's mighty power, I wrote a joyful letter to some Christians living seven miles from here and asked them if they would come over and help us destroy the idols. Ten men responded, and in two days the temple was forever rid of gods made by hands. The wooden ones we split and burned, and the clay ones we beat into dust. There's the garden we made from that dust right over there; we've planted onions and garlic in it. And do you know, Miss Vaughan, the most wonderful thing of all is that crowds of heathen people watched us, and they were not angry at all. They even laughed when we split the old wooden idols limb from limb!"

That night my Bible woman and I slept in that old heathen temple, peaceful in our Saviour's care. I slept on my army cot which I usually carried with me and the others stretched out on boards laid across the benches. They actually preferred hard beds because they were used to them. A brick kang covered with a piece of straw matting is the regulation bed.

Before six in the morning there was a loud knocking at the door. "Who's there?" I called.

"Han Ku Niang," a woman replied, "will you please let us in? We have come to hear you preach the gospel."

"But what brought you so early?" I asked. "We are not up yet."

"Oh, please open the door," came the answer. "There are six of us and we've been up all night grinding grain and making bread for the day, so our mothers-in-law would let us come. Oh, won't you let us in and tell us about Jesus?"

In this way our preaching began at daylight. Ever larger groups of women joined us, until by nine o'clock, the appointed time for our opening service, there was scarcely breathing room in the temple, much less seating capacity.

Throughout the four days of the Conference, from early morning until ten o'clock at night, the six Bible women and I spoke without intermission to the women packed inside the temple. The pastor and four evangelists were preaching to the men outside, where the audience was so great that the "graves of the gods" had to be used for standing room. Out in the streets crowds of both men and women listened eagerly to whatever the Christian laity could give to them.

We took our meals, for the most part just bread and tea, between sentences while we taught. Only at supper time did the crowds thin sufficiently to let us eat in comparative comfort.

The official who had been so kind to our people attended one service with his secretaries. He sent his wives to our women's meeting in company with their slaves and children.

To say that there were many additions to the church in those meetings is to give only a poor, inadequate idea of the blessing poured out in those four days.

And some time, I hope, the Lord will permit me to complete the work on the foundation laid at that wonderful Conference.

Chapter XVIII

"God's Gift"

MANY CHRISTIANS long, as they read the Bible, for miracles such as those recorded in the Word of God to happen in their own lives, thinking that if such wonders occurred they would at once trust God implicitly. "For instance the story in Genesis, of Isaac's miraculous birth." They wait and wait, and long with great longings, for something to happen, and finally agree with the unbelievers that God works differently in the twentieth century than He did in those early years. The simplicity of faith never becomes real to such; because they wait "to see" before believing God's word, not realizing that seeing is not believing. (Heb. 11-1.)

How refreshing the simple trust of many a lowly Chinese believer in contrast!

In the village of Yuen Kia lived a family of seven; the father and mother with five daughters. They were Christians, but though they knew the Lord and had received His peace, they felt that their happiness was incomplete without a son and heir. The family

owned quite a piece of land, and were considered in their community as well able to eat good food and wear comfortable clothes,
which in China, "that land of grinding poverty," meant wealth.

I visited this village at the invitation of Pastor Chao, and found
it a fine centre of Christian influence, with the "Yuen" family as
leaders in all church activities. Mrs. Yuen was not different from
the ordinary Chinese Christian woman I found in every village.
She could not read; neither could she write; she had no education
of any kind. Her youngest daughter was at that time ten years
old, and she herself over forty-five. In accordance with the natural laws of our being, she had some years before given up all
hope of ever having a son, and consequently had mourned griev-
ously over her disgrace. For it is a disgrace in China to have no
son to carry on the family name.

SCRIPTURE TESTIMONY
The believer is to be
persistent in prayer
LUKE 11:5-10

While I visited in this
community we held meet-
ings each day and the power
of God was upon us here,
as elsewhere during those
years of revival. Without any
outward sign, as dew on the grass, a new revelation of power
in and through the Lord Jesus Christ, came to this father and
mother during these services. Without a word to each other,
without a word to any one else, in the secret recesses of each
heart they waited on God for "their hearts' desire." (Psi. 37-4-5.)
Mrs. Yuen took me aside, drew me to the inner courtyard of their
home, while with shining face she pointed to the little hidden
nook in the yard where she had "three times a day" poured out
her petition to her Lord "for a son."

A year later a son was born to these parents. Their joy knew
no bounds. They sent for Pastor Chao.

"How can we name this child which God has given us ? Tell us what we shall call him."

"If he is sent from God, then call him 'God's Gift,'" said the Pastor; "what could be more befitting!" So then and there he was named "Tien shi," which means Heaven's Gift.

Will this name not be a testimony to God's power throughout all the years of this boy's life?

Scripture Testimony Index

Louisa Vaughan's very first experience in ministry to women in China was discouraging. The prospect of teaching illiterate women, who were completely occupied with the tasks of daily life, seemed impossible. When Ms. Vaughan took the matter to God in prayer, He spoke the promise of John 14:13-14, and her burden rolled away. She had merely to ask in His name and trust Him for the outcome.

Mrs. Wang was a woman whose husband reviled and cursed her for six months. But instead of responding in kind, she constantly prayed that God would forgive him...because he didn't understand. One day God answered her prayers, and her husband was truly converted.

Holy Spirit directs believers in ministry
Matthew 10:19-20 · Acts 8:29 · Acts 13:2 · Acts 15:28 ·
Acts 16:6-10 · Acts 20:22 · Romans 8:14

Holy Spirit convicts people of their sin................................ 13
John 16:8

In a conference meeting, Miss Vaughan was led by the Holy Spirit to ask everyone to stop and pray a specific prayer. As they obeyed this leading of God, the Holy Spirit fell upon them with great power and conviction.

Generously give to those in need.. 18
Acts 4:32-37 · Galatians 6:2 · Hebrews 13:16 · 1 John 3:17

Miss Vaughan writes about a great revival among the Chinese Christians. Men and women alike were confessing their sins of covetousness and then giving liberally of their time, experience, and material wealth for the advancement of God's cause.

Deliverance from enemies and circumstances.................... 21
Luke 1:71

Louisa Vaughan's cook, Shao Wei Chao, fell in with bad company who convinced him to leave her employ and seek a dubious opportunity. Miss Vaughan spent three days praying for her cook's deliverance from this plan. God answered her prayers and the boat carrying Shao Wei Chao was turned back by a terrible storm.

God answers prayer
Luke 18:7 · John 15:7 · Acts 12:5 · James 5:15

Don't be anxious, instead make requests known
to God 23
Philippians 4:6

While on a journey with "friends," Shao Wei Chao was deceived and robbed of all his belongings, leaving him stranded in a strange land. In his confusion, he was reminded by the Holy Spirit to pray. He prayed for help, and what happened was clearly God's mighty help.

Holy Spirit convicts people of their sin
John 16:8

Luke 6:38

Mr. Swen, a Chinese farmer, was convicted of his sins and he publicly confessed them, promising to renew his commitment as a servant of God. As he matched his words with actions he saw, like never before, God's powerful blessing on his business.

Luke 6:38

Mr. Swen was enjoying an increasingly bountiful harvest from his farm as he faithfully gave a tenth of each harvest like he promised. But soon, he gave in to covetousness and stopped giving like he had promised. The result was a woeful harvest.

Matthew 10:14 · Mark 6:11 · Luke 9:5

Louisa Vaughan and her assistants had arrived in a village to conduct revival services. Their host was inhospitable, and the place smelled of opium, so the group knelt in prayer to ask God what they should do. The revival band decided to leave, which angered their host. But when he randomly opened his Bible, he landed on Matthew 10:14 and realized that Miss Vaughan was shaking the dust from her feet. This broke the heart of the host and ignited a widespread revival.

Holy Spirit convicts people of their sin 35
John 16:8

Before the revival meetings, a spiritually asleep village church was unwilling to support a school for girls. But on the tenth day of a conference, a backslidden evangelist came under Holy Spirit conviction. His public repentance led to a revival amongst the congregation. Echoing Psalm 110:3, "That His people will be willing in the day of His power," the school was enthusiastically supported.

Disciples must keep their word 39
Matthew 5:37

Miss Vaughan and Mr. Leng's family agreed to pray every day for Mr. Leng, a backslidden evangelist on death row for the crime of vandalism—specifically for sharing in the looting of the Imperial Palace. After over a year of keeping to their word to pray, Mr. Leng was delivered in an unusual way.

God, with great demonstration of love, forgives the truly repentant 42
Luke 15:11-31

Chinese farmer, Chang Fang Yuan, heard the story of The Prodigal Son from Miss Louisa Vaughan in a tent meeting. Chang had attended simply to hear a white woman speak Chinese, but by the end he saw himself as the Prodigal and begged to know how to get back to his Heavenly Father. This farmer was converted and boldly returned to his village in spite of the promise of great persecution.

Believers will suffer terrible things for the sake of Jesus' name
Matthew 24:9-14
Father forgive them, for they know not what they do
Luke 23:34 · Acts 7:60
Counted worthy of suffering disgrace for the Name......... 44
Acts 5:41

Chinese farmer, Chang Fang Yuan, was nearly beaten to death for preaching the Gospel in his village. He didn't die, but instead he prayed to his Heavenly Father for the forgiveness and salvation of his attackers. His prayers were answered.

Ask Me anything in My name... 47
Matthew 18:19 · John 14:13-14 · John 16:23-24

Louisa Vaughan's "one method of work" was to pray with complete reliance upon the promise of John 14:13-14. When faced with a particularly difficult situation of presenting the Gospel to a highly distracted young mother, she simply asked for her conversion in the name of Jesus. In answer to prayer God glorified Himself in the woman's thorough conversion.

God gave a glimpse of what is to come............................. 49
2 Corinthians 12:2

Mrs. Jang died and saw heaven. The next day she was miraculously brought back to life to share with her family and many who flocked to listen to her stories of heaven. While there, the Heavenly Father told her to return to her people, but that He would take her back on the 12th day of the following month. On the appointed day, Mrs. Jang happily went back to God.

Holy Spirit convicts people of their sin
John 16:8
The prayer of a person in right relationship with God is effective
James 5:16-18

James 5:17

The people of Shan Tung province were desperate for rain. For weeks they made sacrifices and offered prayers to their rain god, but to no avail. Ultimately, giving up, they threw the idol in a ditch. At the same time the Christians of the area had been praying for rain and were discouraged that their prayers also brought no rain. In a purposefully public demonstration of James 5:16-18, Miss Vaughan led the believers to seek right relationship with God through repentance, which resulted in a dramatic answer to prayer.

Signs and wonders draw attention to Gospel message
John 4:28-29 · Acts 8:5-8

Acts 9:35 · Acts 9:42

The chief official of a village was so opposed to the Christian doctrine that he had made believing or teaching it to be a capital offense. But after witnessing the clear deliverance of a demon-possessed man, the villagers begged to hear the Gospel, and many were converted.

Demons cast out in Jesus' name
Matthew 8:16-17 · Matthew 8:28-32 · Matthew 9:32-34 · Mark 1:23-26 · Mark 9:20-27 · Luke 10:17

Acts 10:19-20 · Acts 11:12

Louisa Vaughan insisted that a deranged woman was mentally ill, not demon possessed. However, the fact that the woman was nearly physically incapable of saying the name of Jesus, combined with the fact that Miss Vaughan and her fellow workers independently heard the same thing from the Lord that "This kind goeth not out but by prayer and fasting," convinced Miss Vaughan to recognize the woman's true condition.

God communicating in a dream..**76**
Matthew 1:20 · Matthew 27:19 · Acts 2:17

Two men who had nearly killed their widowed aunt were independently visited by the same dream, on the same night, in which Jesus warned them to repent or perish by the sword. This dream corresponded exactly to the prayers of the church inspired by Exodus 22:22-24 which says, "Ye shall not afflict any widow...I will kill you with the sword..."

Ask Me anything in My name...**81**
Matthew 18:19 · John 14:13-14 · John 16:23-24

A Chinese church was attacked over a child's desecration of a pagan temple. In the conflict, a persecutor was shot in the arm and falsely accused the pastor of the act, producing a gun with the pastor's name on it as evidence. There was little hope of justice from the non-Christian official, but the believers stood on the promise of John 14:13-14 and prayed. God moved the official to examine the evidence impartially.

True disciples forsake the old self and put on the new self...**84**
Ephesians 4:20-27 · Ephesians 4:28-5:9 · Ephesians 5:10-20 · Colossians 3:5-17

Louisa Vaughan prayed for a new cook, whom God provided in the person of a profligate young man with a notorious reputation for vice. At first she resisted, but he said that he wanted to learn to be good, and that she was known for teaching people how. Within a week he met the Lord Jesus and was completely transformed. He had been made good, and he went home to his people, a changed man.

Unbelievers pleading to hear the Gospel............................ 87
Acts 16:9-10

Louisa Vaughan's cook had been so dramatically changed by the Gospel, that his village elders wanted to learn the secret. Like the Macedonian that the Apostle Paul saw in a vision, they pleaded with her saying, "Please come over and help us, we are hungry to learn."

All great movements of God are birthed in prayer............ 95
Acts 1:14

The Christians of Lao Shan Wei earnestly desired revival in their community, so like the Apostles devoted to prayer in the upper room in Jerusalem before the outpouring of the Holy Spirit, as described in the second chapter of Acts, the Chinese believers prayed for a whole year. And then the revival came.

God leads believers in opposition to idolatry
Acts 17:16-17 · 1 Corinthians 8:4 · 1 John 5:21
God answers prayer... 97
Luke 18:7 · John 15:7 · Acts 12:5 · James 5:15

The believers of Lao Shan Wei had been praying specifically for a place to hold revival meetings as their little church was too small to hold those who had already expressed a desire to attend. Not only did God answer their prayers, but He did so by casting the idols out of a large temple building.

The believer is to be persistent in prayer............................**102**
Luke 11:5-10

Mrs. Yuen was persistent, praying three times a day in her inner courtyard for a son to be born to her and her husband. In time they joyfully welcomed a baby boy named "Tien shi," which means "Heaven's Gift."

Walking Together Press is a non-profit publishing
company devoted to supporting grassroots libraries
in Africa through global book sales and through
providing free library editions.

To read our story, to see our catalog, and to learn
more about how you can help us in our mission,
visit our website at:

https://walkingtogether.press

www.ingramcontent.com/pod-product-compliance
Lightning Source LLC
Chambersburg PA
CBHW031423120626

46545CB00006B/2245